*Me' xhe ciya a Diène N'dour a livre a leke
binduma mi Kuumba N'dour.*

For Diène—
You taught me to believe.

Population and Ethnic Groups of Senegal

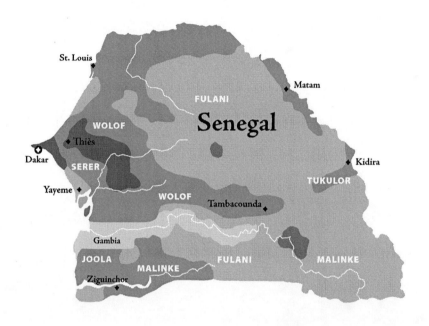

St. Louis

Matam

FULANI

Senegal

WOLOF

Thiès

Dakar

SERER

Kidira

Yayeme

TUKULOR

WOLOF

Tambacounda

Gambia

JOOLA

FULANI

MALINKE

MALINKE

Ziguinchor

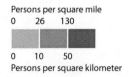

Persons per square mile
0   26   130

0   10   50
Persons per square kilometer

GLOSSARY

Frequently Used Words in Wolof, Serer, Arabic, and French

Assalam alaikum *Arabic*

Hello—*Literally: Peace onto You*

Attaya *Wolof*

Traditional Senegalese tea

Baobab *Wolof*

A native tree with a thick trunk and gourdlike fruit used in juice

Begg nga cebb *Wolof*

You like rice—*A common joke, a way to call someone gluttonous*

Bissap *Wolof*

Hibiscus leaves used for juice

Booboo *Wolof*

Formal outfit consisting of a long tunic and pants (for men) or loose fitting tunic and skirt (for women)

Campement *French*

Hotel or hostel with basic accommodations, including campsites

Ceeb *Wolof*

Rice

Ceeb bu jeen *Wolof*

Rice and fish, traditional dish of Senegal

CFA *French, Wolof*

Communauté Financière Africaine franc—the currency of Senegal

Dedet *Wolof*

No

Gere meke *Serer*

Come here

Inshallah *Arabic*

God willing

Jamm rekk *Wolof*

Peace only

Japalé gouné *Wolof*	Lending a hand to children
Jerejef *Wolof*	Thank you
Joola	The language of a Senegalese ethnic group with the same name
Le cyber *French*	Internet café with computers available for a hourly fee
Maangi fii rekk *Wolof*	I am here, only
Ndank, ndank *Wolof*	Step by step
Ndigendiaye *Wolof*	A large bus that seats thirty passengers
Nga def? *Wolof*	How are you? (What's up?)
Nit nit ay garabam *Wolof*	Man is man's best remedy
Ño ko bokk *Wolof*	You are welcome (Literally: we share it)
Sept-place *French*	A taxi that seats seven
Serer	The language of an ethnic group with the same name
Talibé *Wolof*	Child beggars
Teranga *Wolof*	Hospitality
Toubab *Wolof*	Foreigner
Waaw *Wolof*	Yes
Waay *Wolof*	An interjection used for emphasis
Wah ker ga *Wolof*	Family (Literally: People of the house)
Wolof	The language of an ethnic group with the same name
Xaa *Serer*	No

Contents

11 INTRODUCTION

17 POWER OF THE PEN

LESSON ONE
21 *Ño ko bokk*—We share it
+ Caught with My Hand in the Cookie Jar
+ Brotherly Love
+ Unwelcome Hospitality

LESSON TWO
49 *Ndank, ndank*—Step by step
+ Just on Time
+ Ndank, Ndank
+ Hurry Up and Wait

LESSON THREE
67 *Nit nit ay garabam*—Man is man's best remedy
+ My Cousin, the Fat Pig
+ Homesick

LESSON FOUR
87 *Inshallah*—God willing
+ Inshallah
+ Grapefruit Calendar
+ Women's Work
+ Telecommunications

LESSON FIVE

121   *Jal Ki Jegg*—Work it, have it
   + A Walk on the Beach
   + The Talibé
   + Visiting L'Ecole de Primaire de Point E
   + An Answer
   + A Dakar Reunion, a Dakar Good-bye

LESSON SIX

157   *Faydah*—A sense of self
   + The First Rain
   + Love
   + Land of the Lonely
   + Power of the Pen Redux

183   **EPILOGUE**

Introduction

If there is a secret to happiness, the Senegalese know it. During moments that I lived there, I often found myself pausing to look up to count the people I saw smiling. Whether shaking it to *mbalax* music at an impromptu dance party, walking through the tear gas of student strikes, or squeezing nine people in a car built for seven on a thirty-hour ride, I could always find someone whose face was lit up with a smile.

The only exception to this rule was when I was hanging out with large groups of other Americans. We would sit around and talk about the unbearable heat and insatiable mosquitoes. Our stories were shows of one-upmanship. A nightmare story of indigestible palm oil was nothing to compare to one of lying awake all night listening to the bleating of a neighbor's insomniac goat. Our shared joy was in practicing the delivery of the survival stories we would impress friends and family with back home. Day by day, our armor against Africa, against Senegal, built of first aid kits, hand sanitizer, Mefloquine anti-malarial pills, and emergency stashes of Xanax, was thinning quicker than we imagined. At some point, we would have to make a choice. Surrender or go home. Meanwhile, the Senegalese were living the life we were barely surviving and living it well. In their company, I was laughing more, hurrying less, and handing control of my fate over to the divine.

As an outsider, I spent months pondering the formula for their pandemic *joie de vivre* and searching for the fabled African wiseman to reveal it to me. Some parts of the equation are clear. Spending most of your time with family and friends. A national commitment to welcoming other people into your life. Smiling at one another. Encouraging others to feel at peace. Giving every person you meet enough time to update you on the well-being of their family. Those are at least a few of the first steps.

I didn't sit down and write this book from start to finish, but rather spent four years telling stories about my year in Senegal to Rotary Clubs and college students across Wisconsin, the Midwest, and even the country. I first went to Senegal as a Rotary Ambassadorial Scholar, which granted me a year of funding for post-graduate study. In return, I shared a commitment to the scholarship's mission of furthering international understanding and friendly relations among people of different countries. When I got back home, I talked to as many Rotary clubs as I could to thank them for the opportunity of a lifetime. I still do. In writing those thirty-minute speeches, I wrote this book, story by story.

During those speeches, themes that I did not expect presented themselves. Learning a culture through language. The evolution of Project Japalé Gouné, from an idea shared among three Rotary Scholars to a nonprofit organization that serves 10,000 lunches each year to poor students in Dakar, Senegal. Proverbs and lessons that buttressed the Rotary International motto of "Service Above Self." The idea that nothing ever goes according to plan.

My plan, laid out in my scholarship application, was to go back to school to get my Master's in Economics and work for international human rights organizations. Senegal entered my plan in the final stages. As a little girl, I would spin a dusty globe in our basement, then drag my index finger along it until it came to a stop. Whichever country was under the white of my nail was where I was fated to travel some day. Senegal never came up under my fingernail. In fact, it didn't come into my mind until I was researching potential study institutions for my application to the Rotary Foundation, opened *AFRICAN HIGHER EDUCATION: An*

International Reference Book and saw that there was a university in Dakar, Senegal, with a Center for Human Rights Research. I promptly pulled out an atlas and looked for Senegal on the map. *The west coast? That means spoken French and a beach. Sign me up.*

As soon as I was awarded the scholarship, I hurried to make a plan that would maximize the benefit of an additional year of post-graduate study. Before I had even arrived in Senegal, I had con-tacted a graduate school in the UK that said they would give me credit towards a Master's for some of my university classes and more if I did a volunteer internship in Senegal. When my plane touched down in Dakar, the capital of Senegal, I felt well-equipped to follow my plan.

Those plans unraveled before I could adjust to the sub-Saharan heat.

The Senegalese would tell me that my first mistake was putting too much faith in my own plan. *Man plans, God decides,* they say. My second mistake was hurrying through my days, trying to check tasks off my to-do list. Instead, be at peace. Slow down and let life unfold before you, step by step.

Coming from the United States, where people believe they can plan their days down to the minute and then rely on electronic de-vices to remind them of each segmented part of their plan, this shift was not easy to make. If I were to redirect all the energy I spend trying to "get things done," what else would I focus on?

Friends and family, the Senegalese would tell me. Why all this time spent concerned about moving up? Towards what? More money? More recognition? Anything worth having and any place worth going is best shared. Take that energy and focus it on *wel-coming people into your life* and *sharing* what you can with them.

Even while my plans to perfect my French were ousted by the fact that everyone spoke Wolof to each other, and while the start of my graduate classes was pushed back months, I clung to the idea that my trip needed a definitive purpose. I searched for one everywhere: in French and Wolof classes, on public transportation, in rural villages without electricity or running water, and through bouts of paralyzing homesickness. I pleaded with Destiny through my journal writing, asking her to show herself before I stopped believing in her. On the really bad days, I simply spent hours writing in my journal about how I had nothing more meaningful to do than writing in my journal.

Eventually, I did. Something meaningful beyond what I could have dreamed. In hindsight, I can see how I needed some time to make it happen, to let things fall in place and the stars align. In those sweaty moments, though, I rushed between ideas and inspirations, replacing meaning with speed. I couldn't help it; this is what it means to be American. As workers, we expect to move up quickly. As consumers, we demand faster technology. As families, we schedule ourselves into a breakneck pace.

It wasn't until my Wolof teacher told me that time does not exist that I was able to begin my concession. With no other options, I dropped my agenda and started to roll with the punches, taking life one step at a time. If I did this long enough, my teacher promised me, I could catch any monkey in the West African jungle.

I kept my compass pointed at a year of invaluable learning experiences and meaningful service, but gave up trying to steer along the exact course I plotted. Soon, I began to notice that people and situations along the new route presented me with opportunities that I could never have found using my own map. Before I knew it, there was no trace of my original route, but what had arrived were this book and a school lunch program in Dakar. The best part is, I now understand that the journey is not over.

In writing this book, I hope to do three things. First, I intend to share the lessons I learned from the Senegalese with the hope that by integrating them into our lives, we find ourselves a little happier each day and a little wiser about the reality of Africa. From our comfortable distance across the Atlantic, we tend to lump all fifty-three countries of Africa together as a continent of despair. In the media, as in our minds, Africa is represented by images of famine, genocide, AIDS, and brutality. I want to create images that mirror what I saw: hospitality, wisdom, brilliant linguists, progress, peace. I cannot represent the entire continent, but only the country of Senegal, and the Wolof and Serer people who live there and in the neighboring West African nations.

Second, I want to share how the ideas in these lessons nurtured Project Japalé Gouné from the seedling of an idea into a nonprofit that helps feed over 10,000 hungry minds each year.

Finally, this book is a long thank-you letter to Rotarians around the world who gave me (and give thousands of other students each year), the opportunity to promote goodwill and international understanding around the world during a year as Rotary Ambassadorial Scholars. The best way I know to express my gratitude is by telling stories.

This book only scratches the surface of the wisdom passed down for generations to the lucky few living in Senegal today. I owe everything I learned to the people I met along the way.

I eventually did meet the wiseman (and you will too, in Chapter 9 on Christmas Day) and recently one night at dinner, I asked him point blank.

"What is this Senegalese secret to happiness?" I asked.

"It is simple," he said. "We wake up each morning and the first thought we focus on is to thank God."

Stop right there. My first thought of the day is usually, "That d*&n alarm clock already?!" The only thing I thank God for is the snooze button.

"Thank Him for what?" I asked. "The day hasn't even started yet."

"For waking me up. For giving me another day," he said. "From that gratitude comes the promise that I will do my best to make it a good one, in hopes of being rewarded with tomorrow."

In that vein, I write with gratitude to you for reading my story. I will do my best to make it a good one.

The Power of the Pen

I know what I am about to do could flag me as a terrorist. It is exactly what the Federal Transportation Authority has instructed me *not* to do each time I fly. I am standing in JFK's terminal waiting to check into my international flight to Dakar, Senegal, and a strange woman is trying to persuade me to take an item from her luggage and put it in my own.

Just minutes ago, this 50-year-old woman, dressed in a bright, multicolored batik dress, had me feeling like we were friends. I watched her befriend all the others waiting in line, including a man she asked to watch her bags while she took her prayer mat to the waiting area, faced it towards Mecca, and prostrated herself in prayer. It was when she came back and I overheard her thank the temporary guardian in Wolof that I got the courage to say "hello," or in Wolof, *assalam alaikum*.

Much to my delight, I made it through the entire traditional greeting, even though I had not spoken a word of Wolof for two months. Such is the power of repetition; I had said that greeting dozens of times each day, every day, during my original eight months in Senegal. It may have been buried in the recesses of my mind, but it surfaced without much conscious effort.

When we finished our conversation, the woman clapped her hands and laughed and said she couldn't believe it: a *toubab*, or foreigner, who spoke Wolof.

Now, without taking a breath after laughing, she leans over to ask me a favor.

"Mademoiselle." As she says it, the smile melts from her face, giving it a sense of grave urgency. "I have a problem."

I know this familiar dialogue. It always presents a problem, never requests help.

"What is it?" I ask. "Maybe I can help you in some way."

"I have too much luggage. Gifts for my family, gifts for my friends. I will surely have to pay for the extra weight." She stands over her bulging suitcases, colossal squares of cheap canvas fabric nearly ripping at the seams, cinched in the middle by a wide vinyl strap. I feel her pain; even though my return trip to Senegal is only for three weeks, I, too, have filled my bags with gifts. Still, the most important gifts I will be sharing are not something I have in my suitcase.

She eyes my two suitcases: a tall camper's backpack and a wide black duffel bag, shrunken and shriveled next to hers.

"Could you take some things for me? Otherwise I pay." She is smiling broadly, as though it has already been decided in her favor and we are simply working out the details. And sure enough, in my heart, I have decided; I can't refuse her. This is the magic of the Senegalese: act so kind to strangers that you need not even ask a favor before they are offering to do it, believing it was their idea in the first place.

"Okay," I say, eyeing the airline employees who have booted up the computers and begun checking in passengers. "Just give me a few things."

She unbuckles the seatbelt-like strap and flips open her suitcase, unabashedly handing the contents to me. She pushes a stack of a dozen brightly colored T-shirts, all with I ♥ NYC screenprinted in black on the front, into my hands. A vision takes me to her family's home where everyone is sitting around making *attaya*, traditional Senegalese tea, listening to her stories of adventures in America, dressed in matching T-shirts.

The T-shirts pretty much fill my bag, so I zip it back up and wait for the line to start moving. When I finally get to the counter, the airline employee goes through her usual security screening questions.

"Have any strangers asked you to carry items for them or given you something to put in your luggage?" she asks.

"No," I answer confidently. After all, there are no strangers in Senegal.

* * *

When our plane lands in Dakar, I look out the tiny window at the ground crew wheeling the staircase over to the plane's door. When it is my turn to exit down those stairs, I pass the turbines of the jet engine, which are taller than I am, and underfoot the metal stairs creak as I descend onto Senegalese soil.

Only an hour after sunrise, I can already feel the dry heat creeping in and see it rising off the tarmac in waves. Once I start sweating, I probably won't stop until I get back on the air-conditioned plane to go home.

Before I am allowed entry to the country, I must convince a dusty old customs bureaucrat that I am worthy of passage. I eye the inspector sitting in the booth at the front of my line. He is dressed in a faded tan military uniform complete with a beret, a relic of the French occupation. His lips are pursed as he gazes over the stack of dusty papers and a big red stamp in his booth. Salt-stained wet patches are growing under both of his arms, fueled by the extra weight he carries in his paunch belly.

He seems out of place, here in the oldest democracy in West Africa, 44 years after independence, dressed in a French-style military uniform. When the man in front of me shows his Senegalese passport and is reprimanded by the inspector, the two of them have a heated verbal exchange in Wolof. They are talking fast and simultaneously, making it impossible for me to understand. The conversation ends abruptly when the inspector snaps closed the passenger's passport and passes it back under the glass partition.

A tall slender man of about 40, the passenger reaches into his breast pocket and pulls out a handkerchief, blotting the sweat off his forehead. Then, he reaches back into the pocket and pulls out a package of pens.

I recognize them instantly as UniBall Vision pens from home, but even if I was not an aficionado, there is no doubting that these are an American item; the over-packaging is a dead giveaway. Each pen is individually wrapped in a plastic display box, the dozen smaller boxes are in a larger clear plastic box, and that is wrapped in plastic. The outside wrapping crinkles as he slides it through the small opening under the glass partition.

The customs official turns the package over several times in his hands, giving it the same scrupulous inspection he gives countless passports each day. Finally, with a decisive nod, he puts the package below the shelf, out of view. He takes out his big red stamp, finds a blank page in the man's passport, and gives him the stamp of approval into the country.

I am not surprised by the power of the pen in Senegal. After all, it is what has brought me back.

LESSON 1

Ño ko bokk
We share it
Wolof

In Senegal, the land of teranga (hospitality),
anything worth having is worth sharing.
In giving, we double our joys and halve our sorrows.
Project Japalé Gouné was born as an answer to
the simple question of what we could best share.

CHAPTER 1

Caught with My Hand in the Cookie Jar

Brigitte has caught me red-handed. I've been exposed as a selfish liar by a 12-year-old girl. I see her in the doorway of my bedroom, and her big brown eyes look at me quizzically. She has her school notebook in one hand and a shiny new Bic pen tucked behind her ear. I want to open my mouth to explain, but I can't speak without spraying crumbs all over her. I have committed one of the cardinal sins of Senegalese culture: I have something wonderful and have kept it all to myself.

It was a long day and I went to the corner boutique to pick up some comfort food: chocolate chip cookies. The problem is that I wanted to keep them to myself, hoarding the package so it would last a few days. I've been trying for a week to be more Senegalese: speaking Wolof, spending all my time with my host family, and adopting the open closet policy for everything I own. Exhausted by the effort, I came home from class and lied; I said I had a headache and shut myself in my bedroom so I alone could witness my gluttony.

For a moment, as melted chocolate oozed onto my fingers and dripped down my chin, I was on familiar territory: alone, enjoying junk food, and not having to share anything. Recharging my American batteries. I closed my eyes and imagined myself at home, where everyone speaks my language and asks before borrowing things. I was far from here. So far, in fact, that I didn't hear Brigitte tap softly on my bedroom door.

It all began this morning, when I was jolted upright in my bed by a siren. A man's voice was projected throughout the neighbor-hood through a scratchy bullhorn. My heart began to speed up with thoughts of an inclement weather alert system or an emer-gency evacuation of the city. It was dawn and my bedroom was still dark so my hands scrambled across my bedside table search-ing for my glasses, sending pens, notebooks, and my alphabetized Wolof vocabulary flash cards rattling to the floor. Before I found my glasses, I recognized the chorus of the man's words.

"*Allaaaaaaahhh Akhbar. Allaaaaaaaaaaaah Ahkbar.*" God is great, in Arabic. The muezzin, a man chosen to lead the call to prayer, was shouting from the top of the *Mosque de Karak's* minaret, hastening the devout to their prayer mats. Each morning for the last week, the same guy had woken me up with the same call. Each night, I'd fallen asleep reminding myself what to expect the next morning, but my exhaustion at the end of each day was so deep that waking up felt like pulling myself from quicksand. My mind was saturated with Wolof vocabulary and French grammar, leaving no space for the reminder to ignore the call to prayer and take advantage of another hour of sleep.

This morning, I rolled over, put my pillow over my head, and tried to fall back asleep. But it was too late. Sweat was already beading down my neck onto the six-inch-thick foam pad I'd been euphemistically calling a mattress. It was damp and flattened under my weight, offering little cushion from the hard plywood of my bed frame. After accepting the inevitable early morning rise, I heard the others in the house up and moving. I debated which was more distressing: having to get out of bed or knowing that the past exasperated twenty minutes were the only alone time I would have all day.

I moved in with my host family, the Colys, a week ago, days after arriving in Dakar, Senegal. They live in Karak, a wealthy sub-urb of the capital city where families are fortunate enough to afford homes with running water, three square meals a day, electricity, re-frigerators, indoor bathrooms, and televisions. These are luxuries out of the reach of most of their fellow countrymen.

Ours is a one-story cement house with three bedrooms, a living room, a kitchen, two small bathrooms, and a small tiled courtyard where the maid hangs laundry and washes the dishes. There are so many people living in the house that I am still unsure how (and if) they are all related.

The matriarch of the family is a broad woman with an infectious smile whose entire body shakes when she laughs. Everyone in the house calls her *Mami Chou*, Mommy Dearest. At 60 years of age, she buzzes around all day: teaching classes at a Catholic school, cooking dinner, washing laundry, and demanding that Brigitte and Claude, the school-aged children in the house, study diligently.

Brigitte is a precocious 12-year-old with cocoa skin and black hair braided in cornrows. The first night I arrived, she grabbed my hand in the doorway and did not let it go until I went to bed. In the days since, she has become my shadow, by my side everywhere. Claude is a 10-year-old boy with the habit of making bad jokes and running into walls. He wears coke-bottle glasses with purple, plastic frames. The round lenses are scratched to opacity and, as a result, he is always squinting, standing too close, and tripping over people and inanimate objects. Claude and Brigitte are cousins; their parents have sent them to live with Mami Chou, their grandmother, because the schools in Dakar are superior to those in the rural towns where their parents live.

Only one of Mami Chou's children lives in the house: Viviane is a medical student at the Université Cheikh Anta Diop and studying for her final exams. She has a two-year-old daughter, Binata, the baby of the house, lavished with attention by all. Viviane often leaves on the weekends to visit her husband, who lives in another city.

Then there is Lamine, a handsome 24-year-old man who desperately wants to work, cannot find a job, and spends most of his days hanging out at the Cyber Café with his friends or at the beach with his latest American girlfriend. As far as I can tell, he has no blood relation to anyone in the house, but he is treated like family and called son by Mami Chou and brother by all the kids.

There are other, less permanent residents, who play their roles in the family life. *La bonne*, the maid, is a teenage girl from the countryside, whose family sent her to the city in search of work. She found it knocking on Mami Chou's front door one day, and now makes about $40 a month cooking and cleaning a house she does not sleep in. There is another young man who arrives on a red moped every evening at dinnertime, eats with the family, and then leaves for the night. The most jovial part-timer is an old man who comes by almost nightly, dressed in the same long, powder blue tunic and navy vest, smelling of whiskey, and sits in front of the television cracking jokes and making everyone laugh, no one more than Mami Chou.

Finally, there are Stephanie and me: two American students, studying at the same school and sharing a bedroom.

The family speaks Wolof amongst themselves, but for my benefit will speak French with me. I am taking intensive French and Wolof classes in the hopes that I'll get the family's inside jokes.

This morning, as all other mornings, Mami Chou served me a breakfast of baguette with butter and hot water for my Nescafé instant coffee.

"*Katie, fanan ak jamm?*" She asked me if I slept well. As I spooned the teaspoon of sparkling black crystals into my mug, I contemplated my response. I had to think a moment before I spoke. English: "Good, thanks." French: "*Bien, merci.*" Finally, Wolof.

"*Jamm rekk, jerejef,*" I said. My responses to even the most basic questions took so long that I was beginning to feel like that kid seated in the back of the classroom whom the teacher labels special and at whom everyone smiles excessively. As I poured the hot water in my mug and watched the specks of black melt into a pool of brown, I wondered if giving up a year of my life to live in West

Africa as *that* girl was such a good idea.

There are a few signs of hope. After only a week of lessons, a few Wolof words have become reflex responses and I no longer need to translate before using them.

Assalam alaikum. Hello.

Jerejef. Thank You.

Ño ko bokk. You are welcome.

The last one, *ño ko bokk*, is my favorite. The proper response to thank you, but translated literally into *we share it*. Three simple words that perfectly summarize the foundation of the communal life in Senegal. As if all things you have to offer are not exclusively yours, but simply in your guardianship.

Later this morning, I arrived at the *Centre Baobab*, the school that hosts Rotary Scholars, undergraduates from several American universities' exchange programs, missionaries, travelers, and any one else interested in learning French, Wolof, Pulaar, Serer, or several of the other languages spoken in Senegal.

Running late, I hurried through the lobby and outdoor courtyard, barely saying hello to the people I recognized. I stopped at my classroom door, checked my watch, and walked in a full seven minutes late; the classroom was empty.

"Today," Zator said, ten minutes later when he and the only other student, Natalie, had both arrived, "we learn to talk about family." He looked at us expectantly and then took a sip of water from the repurposed whiskey bottle he kept on his desk. He swallowed loudly, the desperate gulping a sign of his age, and then wiped off his mouth and smiled to reveal the gaps in his mouth where teeth once were. He immediately plugged them with his pipe, empty and unlit.

The hope that this lesson would piece together the puzzle of my host family's lineage was dashed during the introduction of new vocabulary.

"Yaay," said Zator, "means mother." Natalie and I repeated *yaay* back at him.

"*Papa* means father."

"*Rakk bu n'gor* means brother."

"*Rakk bu jigeen* means sister."

"*Maag bu n'gor* means brother."

"*Maag bu jigeen* means sister."

"Wait a minute," I interrupted. "Why are there two words for sister?"

"If she is older than you, you must give her, your *rakk*, the respect she deserves. If she is younger than you, she is your *maag*."

We continued to name the roles of extended family: uncle, aunt, and cousin, but I wasn't ready to stop there. Since the Wolof word for family, *wah ker ga*, translates literally to "people at your house," I wanted to be sure I had all my bases covered.

"What about stepmother?" I asked.

"You say *yaay*," answered Zator. "Same thing, really."

"And half-brother?" I asked.

"Is he older or younger?" Zator asked.

"Younger," I said.

"You say, *rakk bu n'gor*, younger brother," he answered.

"I meant half brother," I gently corrected.

"Katie," Zator said, "there is no half in family."

I left class frustrated. How can you define something if the words to describe it do not exist?

* * *

When I got home from class, Brigitte was waiting, ready to hang out. As I reassembled the contents of my bedside table, still strewn across the room from this morning's fiasco, Brigitte sat on Stephanie's bed, talking quickly about her day.

I couldn't hear her through the chorus in my mind, "Just ten minutes alone—what I wouldn't do for just ten minutes of time alone." I twisted one rubber band around my vocabulary flashcards and then another around my dwindling bundle of pens.

"Katie?" Brigitte asked. "I have a problem. Can you help me?"

"What is it, Brigitte?" I asked.

"My pen is running dry and I'm having trouble doing work at school," she answered.

A small price to pay for peace and quiet. I chose a pen from the bunch in my fist and handed it to her.

"Here you go," I said. "Go try it out on your homework."

She held the pen inches from her face, turning it slowly and examining the clear barrel and blue cap like a pawn shop owner determining its value. She took off the cap, opened her left hand, and began drawing blue circles on her palm.

"Thank you, Katie!" she said. "*Jerejef, waay!*"

"*Ño ko bokk,*" I said, my accent making her giggle. As she stood up to leave, my heart lightened with hope for those ten minutes of solitude I craved. A moment later, it sunk when Mami Chou appeared in the doorway, asking about my day at school. I told her we had spent the morning learning family vocabulary.

"Good!" she said. "That is the most important thing."

"Mami Chou," I asked. "how many people in our house are related?"

She looked at me sternly, with disapproval.

"Katie, we never count how many people live in a house," she said. "It is bad luck."

"Why?" I asked.

"Because you never know when you need to add a few." She eyed my suitcase, still half-unpacked. "A family is always growing," she said.

It was then that I excused myself and took my red-hot embarrassment to the corner store in search of chocolate chip comfort. When I got back, I announced a headache. When I was sure the door was latched, I propped the pillow up against the wall and leaned back in my bed, my legs extended in front of me. I pinched the top of the package between my thumbs and forefingers and opened it gingerly. Gooey chocolate was melted to the sides of the plastic wrapper, and I carefully extracted the first cookie and lifted it to my maw, where I let it sit for a moment. Then I chomped through it, and the next three, like a starving animal who has lucked upon a fresh carcass.

Minutes later, I am busted.

"Katie," Brigitte says as her big brown eyes search me from head to toe. "I have a problem. Can you help me?"

Buying myself some time to chew, I motion Brigitte over to sit on the bed next to me and to go on.

"I haven't eaten since lunch," she says. I recognize this to be a teachable moment, an opportunity to lead by example and do the right thing. Accordingly, I do what any older sister would do at such a moment: I bribe. "Brigitte," I say, swallowing the last of my mouthful. "I am glad you came to me. I have one cookie left that I was saving for you. The problem is, there is not enough to share with everyone, so I will give it to you if you promise not to tell anyone, okay?"

She looks at me, looks at the cookie, and sits for a silent minute. I shift my gaze nervously to the door, now a wide-open invitation to anyone in the house. I nudge her hand with the cookie.

Smiling broadly, Brigitte sticks her hand out, palm up.

"OK, Katie."

I place the cookie on the faded blue circles she drew earlier, closing her fingers around it.

"Remember," I whisper. "Don't tell anyone."

"Wow!" she screams. "Katie, this is a *big* cookie!" She skips out of my room and shouts down the hallway. "Claude! Katie gave us a cookie to share."

Claude squeals with excitement. I hear his feet hit the ground and the chair he was sitting on knocked to the ground.

"Cookie!" he yells.

I collapse my head into my hands for a minute and then look up and in the wall mirror. The melted chocolate that was on my fingers has now smeared all over my face, in case the selfishness was not humiliating enough. I cringe to hear Brigitte moving into the kitchen.

"Mami Chou! Look at the cookie that Katie gave us."

I grab my towel hanging over my dresser and wipe my face clean. I am stuck in place, shame making me immobile. Within moments, Claude is in the doorway, holding a piece of cookie centimeters from his glasses.

"*Jerejef*, Katie," he says. "This looks good."

Now Mami Chou stands behind him, filling the doorframe.

"*Jerejef*, Katie," she says as she pops the morsel into her mouth.

Brigitte squeezes between the two of them, making her way next to me, wrapping herself around my legs.

"*Jerejef*, Katie." She lets go of my leg and breaks the pathetic little remainder of cookie she has left into two, handing half of it up to me.

"Here, Katie," she says. "We'll share it."

"*Jerejef*, Brigitte." I say.

"*Ño ko bokk*," she replies.

CHAPTER 2

Brotherly Love

I t's late one Saturday afternoon and Lamine, Claude, and I are lying on Claude's mattress, flipping through the pages of Lamine's photo album. The first dozen pictures are of his family: a sun faded photo of his father, a cousin wearing a military uniform down on one knee holding a rifle, several group shots of women dressed in their best at a baptism back home. As we continue our way through the album, the photos evolve and the faces become familiar. Lamine in pictures with friends that I know from the neighborhood, seated at a table, drinking bottles of Coca Cola and Flag beer. One photo of Lamine and Paul, who is now dating my roommate, Stephanie, dressed in *booboos*, formal long tunics and cotton pants, and sunglasses.

Then, the first *toubab* appears in the album. A 20-year-old white woman sharing a beach towel with a younger Lamine, leaning back on her elbows and smiling from underneath a sunhat. She is in the next picture, too, wearing black sunglasses in the backseat of a taxi next to Lamine. The third, and final, picture of them is a frame of only their faces. Her extended arm and the angle of shot makes it clear that she took the pictures holding the camera in front of them.

"Who is this?" I ask, trying for nonchalance.

"Sarah," he says.

"Is she American?" I ask.

"Yes," he says. "She was our first exchange student."

"She was one of his giiiiiirlfriends," Claude squeals, nose diving into the album to get a closer look.

I know the family has hosted American students before me, but this is the first time I see one. Brigitte has been keeping a numbered list of their names and showed it to me the day that she added my name next to number 13. Then, and now, I felt inexplicably jealous.

Only a few photos later, Sarah is gone and has been replaced by a chubby blond girl with rosy cheeks. In the four photos she shares with Lamine, their body language grows more intimate. His arm around her shoulders. Next, her arm around his waist. Finally, two arms entangled, hands hidden behind their backs.

Every six photos or so, a new American girl replaces the old. Her hair and eye color change, but her Senegalese evolution is a constant. She always gets tanner in the progression of the photos, sometimes after a beet red sunburn. As her skin tone darkens, she sheds her logo T-shirts and jeans for tailored Senegalese dresses and brightly batiked headwraps. Lamine ages through the pictures, but the women do not. They are always 21-year-old juniors in college during their semester abroad, studying at the *Centre Baobab*.

"Lamine," I ask, "have all your girlfriends been American?"

"Pretty much," he says. "One was an Indian girl who grew up in the United States."

"Why don't you date Senegalese women?" I ask. "They will at least be around for longer than a semester."

"Americans are different," he says.

This is true. American women are a unique breed here in Senegal: they are independent, wear skirts and shorts above the knee, drink alcohol recreationally, have plenty of disposable income, and are eager to immerse themselves fully into Senegalese culture. I understand how easily Lamine and his buddies have appointed themselves cultural guides. It is a semester-long gig with no obligation to reup after the four months.

The last group of pictures is with a woman who stands out because of the way Lamine looks at her in the pictures. He pauses a few second longer before turning the pages.

"Who is she?" I ask.

"Lamine loves her!" Claude pipes in. *"Il veut ses bébés!"* He wants her babies, Claude announces.

Lamine shoves Claude, who gets up and leaves the room singing, *"bébés, bébés, bébés."*

We close the album when Mami Chou calls us in for dinner. On the table for me is my specially prepared vegetarian meal. I became a vegetarian on my 22nd birthday because my liberal activist friends finally convinced me that eating lower on the food chain is more efficient and has less negative impact on the environment. My reasons still hold true: a recent article in the *New York Times*, "Rethinking the Meat Guzzler," estimates that 2.2 pounds of beef are responsible for the equivalent amount of carbon dioxide emitted by the average European car every 155 miles, and burns enough energy to light a 100-watt bulb for nearly 20 days.

What I did not realize until leaving the affluence of the United States is what a privilege it is to choose not to eat meat. When I tried to explain my decision to the Senegalese, backed by facts like those above, I got mostly blank stares. After all, 70% of them are farmers for whom livestock means wealth. In Senegal, eating meat is a sign of physical and financial health.

Instead of trying to explain myself using science and facts, I played upon their religious tolerance. In a country of 95% Muslims, some who don't eat pork, no one thought twice about a religious prohibition on diet.

Still, in a country where vegetarianism is a complete anomaly, my prepared meals are less than thrilling. Tonight it will be boiled eggs, canned peas, and rice. I appreciate the special effort Mami Chou makes, but with meals like this, my trips to the corner boutique for late night *pain au chocolat* have been increasingly frequent.

In the corner of the kitchen, the rest of the family is seated in a circle around a big bowl of *ceeb bu jeen*, rice topped with fish, vegetables, and red palm oil sauce. Each adult sits on a small wooden stool and has a spoon; Claude, Brigitte, and Binata squat around the bowl with freshly washed hands.

After dinner, Lamine asks me if I am interested in going out dancing tonight.

"No, thanks," I say. "Brigitte and Claude have promised to help me with my Wolof."

I've found that as kids who are learning French as their second language in school, Claude and Brigitte make excellent Wolof teachers. They are patient with me, forgive my mistakes, and eagerly take on the role of vocabulary coach. Tonight, they are introducing me to names of vegetables because they think this is the only thing I eat.

"Sou-pa-me," Brigitte sounds out slowly. Cabbage. "*Repetez!*"

"Sou-pa-me," I say, the word dripping off my tongue thickly.

"*Encore,*" instructs Claude.

"Sou-pa-me," I repeat. Brigitte looks at Claude and nods.

"*Data,*" says Brigitte. Then slower, "dah-tah."

"Good one," Claude says to Brigitte. His glasses move up the bridge of his nose, moved by his cheeks suddenly puffy with smile.

"Dah-tah," I say.

"*Repetez!*" commands Brigitte.

"Dah-tah." I pause to see the letters in my mind. "Dah-tah." I say it again. The only method I've found remotely reliable in learning a language is to associate the word with an image or phrase in my mind. These mnemonic devices are easier to recall than words alone. For "*data*" I think of a person presenting something wonderful and explaining "tahdah!"; only they reverse the syllables to make it as mundane as a vegetable.

"Dah-tah," I say. The two teachers look at each other and smile. I feel proud of myself when they move on to the next one. I have won their approval.

"*Coy,*" says Brigitte.

"*Coy,*" I say, thinking of the oversized Japanese goldfish. This one will be an easy one to recall.

"*Coy.*" They both laugh, impressed with my perfect pronunciation. Sometimes, it just comes so easily.

The night passes, word by word, until Mami Chou comes into my room and tells the two of them to go to bed.

"You two promised me you would work on your math tonight!" she says, looking over them at me to wink. "I'll wake you up early tomorrow so you can get started on your problem sets."

In the rare quiet of the house, I crawl into bed and begin memorizing my new vocabulary words. *Soupame* is cabbage. *Data. Coy.* I can't remember what the last two mean, so I remind myself to ask Brigitte and Claude tomorrow.

I hear the back door open and recognize the tipsy footsteps of Lamine. Everyone else in the house is sleeping, so he has no choice but to go to bed himself. In a three bedroom house with eight people, the luxury of your own bed is afforded only to the two American guests. Being the oldest male, Lamine gets his own mattress, but not his own room. I hear him pulling a foam mattress out of the bedroom shared by Viviane, Binata, and Claude, dragging it into the living room to his sleeping place.

I get up and go to the bathroom, acting surprised when I see him.

"How was your night?" I ask, walking over to sit next to him on the mattress. I am wearing an old T-shirt, pair of pajama pants, and my glasses, a late-night and early-morning state of fashion that only family is privy to.

"Good," he says. "We're going to the beach tomorrow, if you want to come."

"Cool, thanks," I say, knowing I won't go. I hug my knees to my chest, suddenly wishing I had stayed in my room.

"How was your night?" Lamine asks.

"Good. I learned a lot of new words for vegetables from Brigitte and Claude. Actually, maybe you could help me translate them.

"*Soupame?*" I ask.

"Cabbage," he says.

"*Data?*" He laughs and I can smell alcohol on his breath. He is lying on his stomach, his head propped on his hands. When he laughs, his head falls into the mattress.

"What?"

I can see *d.a.h.t.a.h.* in my mind, and hear someone presenting it without flare. Maybe I accented the wrong syllable.

"Tahdah?" I say. That can't be right. "I don't remember!" I say in frustration. "They said I could buy it at the corner store." This makes Lamine laugh even harder, and now his whole body is shaking.

"I don't know how to translate that into English," he says.

I am embarrassed. My pronunciation must be horrible. I skip *data* and move on to the next. I picture the large orange Japanese gold fish.

"*Coy,*" I say. My confidence makes me speak louder than I meant to; we had been whispering.

"Oh, Katie!" Lamine says. "Shhhhh!" He puts his forefinger up to his lips. "Everyone is sleeping. You don't want to wake your little professors."

"Sorry," I say. Perhaps he's had one too many Flag beers to care about Wolof words right now. "Will you at least tell me if I can buy *coy* at the corner store?"

Lamine looks at me in a way that makes me forget my messy hair, dorky glasses, and baggy pajamas, even if it is just for a minute. He lifts his finger from his lips and places it on mine.

"Katie," he whispers. "You don't need to go to the store to find *coy* tonight." Sensing his boredom, I feel foolish. I tell him so.

"*Desolé!*" I apologize. "*Je suis folle des langues!*" I am crazy about languages!

"*Tu veux faire un follie?*" he asks. For a moment I don't get the pun. *Do you want to do something foolish?* Then, in an instant, I get it, and the heat of embarrassment rises through my neck, turning my face red.

I laugh it off, pretending it was a joke. I bat his hand away from my face playfully and announce I am going to bed.

"Katie," Lamine says. "When you go the boutique tomorrow,

you don't have to ask for those vegetables. Look on the outside wall: you'll see exactly what they are."

* * *

The next day after a lunch of pasta noodles, oil, and onions, I make my usual trip to the corner store for a *pain au chocolat* snack. As instructed, I walk around to the side of the store and look at the concrete wall. I do not see any advertisements as I had expected, but I do see exactly what Lamine was referring to.

Scribbled on the wall, with the artistic ability and inspiration of pubescent teenagers, are dozens of rudimentary sketches depicting the origins of life. Or at least what a 13-year-old understands the production process to look like. To the left of the pictures, I see an equation that makes it all very clear.

Data + Coy = Bébé

It seems Brigitte and Claude were paying attention in math class after all.

CHAPTER 3

Unwelcome Hospitality

A pile of phone numbers is wedged between the pages of my journal, a visual testament to the *teranga*, or hospitality, of which the Senegalese are so fiercely proud.

Welcome a stranger into your life and share what you have, they say, and someday God will reward you. As a traveler, living in this land of hospitality is paradise; as a woman, it is exhausting.

I am unpacking in my new apartment in Dakar, having left Mami Chou's yesterday, after completing the required one-month stay with a host family. My new place is a modest, one room studio with an attached bathroom and small kitchen. The kitchen has a mini-fridge and two-burner gas stove. Like the bathroom at the Coly family's house, the toilet and shower are only feet from each other in the tiny bathroom, but the entire room is tiled in a light blue color that makes me happy.

Before I throw all the phone numbers away, I sit down and flip through the pile of broken promises to call. I find numbers for teenagers, men my father's age, married men, widowers, professors, street vendors, lawyers, waiters, bus passengers, beggars, bankers, and taxi drivers. They were men who approached me everywhere: on the street, in cyber cafés, at the corner boutique, at bus stops. A woman traveling unaccompanied in Senegal, I quickly learned, is a magnet for men wishing to accompany her. Our exchanges would begin in a friendly way, but in a matter of minutes I would find myself dodging personal questions: *Are you married? Do you have a Senegalese boyfriend? Would you like one?*

Why don't you marry me and take me to the United States? Before long, my guard was up nearly all the time. It was difficult to believe that the invitations to dinner, the beach, day trips, or downtown tours were simply hospitable.

There is only one number, in fact, that I actually considered keeping: Amse's. I pluck a folded slip of paper from the stack and open it to see his neatly printed name and number. At the memory of his cheerful face, I smile ruefully.

* * *

Amse. I met him in Marché Sandaga, my least favorite place in Senegal. There, in the heart of downtown Dakar, already-narrow streets are lined with fabric boutiques, electronic equipment stands, wandering fruit sellers, and vendors hovering over three square feet of carefully aligned merchandise. In front of each store, there is an exterior wall of West African men: the vendors and the touts, who offer to bring you to their friends' shops, where they receive a commission on your purchase. Walking past them as a woman and a *toubab*, or foreigner, I often feel as if I am walking the gauntlet. I look straight ahead, avoid eye contact with all people, and try to make it safely to the other end while being bombarded by men who assail me with personal questions meant to win my loyalty and, eventually, either my business or my hand in marriage.

Amse popped out from a fabric store and started off like all the hawkers do. "*Bonjour!* Welcome to Senegal. *Ça va? Nga def?*"

I had found that the best way to make a quick break from the mass of overly aggressive salesmen who volunteer themselves as marriage potential is to tell them that I am going to meet my husband, who works in the city. After lunch near his office, we will go to our friend's shop on the other end of the market. My imaginary afternoon lets the hawkers know that I have lived in Dakar too long to be tricked into a toubab price and that my husband negates any relationship possibilities.

I gave this spiel to Amse and expected him to politely leave, but instead he burst out laughing. Because of my rusty French, I had actually said that I worked in the market, and that I was on my way to the shop of my husband, on the other end.

"I have heard a lot of stories before," he said, "but I have never had a *toubab* tell me that we share a job!" I was embarrassed and wanted to be angry, but his good looks got even better while he laughed. I could not help but smile, and then suddenly we were sharing a moment of genuine laughter. Before leaving that day, I visited his friend's fabric shop, and on my way out Amse accompanied me to the bus stand, where he gave me his phone number and I happily stuffed it into my pocket.

A month went by and I never called Amse. I had grown skeptical of ever developing a real friendship with any of the men I met in Dakar. They seemed to want one of two things: sex or money. *Amse was probably after the same thing,* I thought. *I was just too naive to see it.*

Now I am in my own apartment and I realize I have forgotten about Amse and these other men, whose numbers I toss into the garbage. To finish my cleaning spree, I need to return to Marché Sandaga for some household items. Although I dread having to put on my invisible armor just to buy dish towels and clothespins, I know it is the only place for affordable one-stop shopping. I take a taxi to the Place de L'Indépendence and stop at the ATM. I scold myself for wearing a sundress with no pockets and forgetting my money belt. Plenty of nightmare tales of pickpockets and purse-snatchers at the market normally have me distributing my money strategically—some in my money belt, bra, purse lining, and wallet—but today's outfit leaves me with no choice. All my money will be in my purse. Leaving the ATM, I walk quickly and brace myself for Marché Sandaga. Sure enough, nearly four blocks before I get there, I am spotted.

"*Bonjour!* Welcome to Senegal. *Ça va? Nga def?* My name is Pop." I ignore him, but he continues the one-sided conversation by asking me about my country, my life here in Senegal, and, of course, my marital status. First I try to gently blow him off by giving him disinterested one-word answers, but that does not work. Then I ask him, in no uncertain terms, to leave me alone. He ignores this, too. His personal questions and offers continue to the point of making me uncomfortable. Does he really expect me to tell him whether I have experienced *all* of Senegal's *teranga* yet, or accept his invitation to do so? Finally, I lose my patience. "Go away!" I snap.

He changes from French to broken English, probably to make sure I understand the insult draped in foreign policy analysis. "What? Why you no friend of mine? Why you come here making war? Why no peace? You hate Senegalese people. Americans love war."

Something in me changes when I travel alone. I have an endless reserve of courage to speak my mind and to protect myself. As I get further from my comfort zone, I get more and more courageous. An insult to me will not go unchallenged.

I take off my sunglasses and look Pop straight in the eyes for the first time. "I don't hate Senegalese people, I just hate you, Pop. You have been following me for ten minutes, even though I have asked you to leave me alone. You have been asking me personal questions and making me disgusting offers. You stole all the patience I had, and then insulted me when it was gone. I am here because I love Senegal and its people, but one day I will leave because I hate men like you."

I stun him long enough to get a good five feet in front of him before he catches up with me again. "*Mademoiselle*, I am so sorry. I did not mean to make you hate me. I just want to be your friend. Please, come to my house for tea. You could share lunch with my family and meet my mother. You will see that I am not a bad person."

I tune out his apologies and continue my shopping, ignoring him completely. I walk up to a stand that sells most of the things I need and start reading my list off to the vendor. Pop is still hovering near, standing in a group of men a few feet from me. As I bargain for a decent price, he pipes in a few times to tell the vendor to be nice to me, because I am his "friend."

The vendor and I finally agree on a price, and I open my purse cautiously to get my wallet. I can not find it.

Panic sets in. I check all the purse pockets. Empty.

I take everything out of my bag and shake it. I pat myself down. Nothing.

By now the vendor and the men standing nearby realize what has happened and offer their advice.

"Look around on the ground. Maybe it fell as you were taking things out."

"Where have you been today? Where did you come from?"

"Was there anyone who followed you? Someone who would not leave you alone?"

I look at Pop. Sure, he had bothered me to the point of losing my cool, but I could not remember his getting close enough to reach into my purse.

"Mademoiselle," the man repeats, "did anyone follow you today?"

Sheepishly, I hesitate. Stealing is so socially unacceptable in Senegal that thieves who are caught are sometimes severely beaten by an angry mob of citizen vigilantes. But it was strange how Pop had followed me after I insulted him. Maybe the rejection had made him bitter enough to seek revenge and take what he still could from me. Even more than blaming an innocent person, I hate being taken advantage of.

"The only person who I have talked to today is . . . him," I say, pointing to Pop. My eyes meet his for the second time that day, and instantly I know I am mistaken. He has taken nothing from me but time and patience.

My purse slips off my shoulder. My confidence slumps. I stare down hard, burning an invisible hole in the concrete. Was I really going to have to apologize to this man? He may not have been the vengeful pickpocket I imagined, but he was still an obnoxious merchant with questionable sales techniques. Blaming him was a mistake, though. As I look around the group of a dozen strange men, I realize he is the closest thing I have here to a friend.

"Katie," someone cries from the other side of the street. "Katie! Hello! It has been a long time. Do you remember me?"

Before anyone can react to my accusation, we all turn to see Amse crossing the street towards us.

"Katie. How have you been? What are you doing here?" He smiles brightly at me and I feel a flood of relief about seeing his familiar face. He gestures to Pop. "Have you met my brother, Pop?"

His brother! I sputter for a moment in horrified embarrassment, then begin talking quickly to fill the air, hoping the words of my explanation will push aside those of my accusation. I explain to Amse how I have lost my wallet. How everyone, including Pop, was helping me to find it . . . my words trail off.

"Why don't you let Pop and me retrace your steps with you? Three sets of eyes will be better than one," Amse says cheerfully. He looks at Pop, who smiles at me, nodding.

We walk silently. Pop never gives any hint about the harsh words we exchanged. Instead he keeps his eyes on the street, scanning for my wallet. After an hour of walking, we arrive at the ATM, the starting point of my day. I lean against the wall to rest, defeated.

"Hey, *toubab*," calls out a man. "I've been waiting for you." He strolls over and hands me my wallet. I open it up. It still has all of my credit cards and cash in it. "You dropped it as you rushed out of the ATM booth this morning, and by the time I picked it up, you had already walked out of sight."

Amse and Pop spend the rest of the afternoon with me, helping me find and bargain for all the things I need and hailing a cab for me when I am ready to go. It feels good to be able to trust strangers again. As they help me load my purchases into the cab, I thank them profusely for their generosity. Before I step in, I turn and face Pop, searching for the right words. Pop waves his hands, silencing me. He and Amse are just sharing with me Senegal's *teranga*, he explains.

"*Teranga* is considered a long-term investment. If you welcome a person into your life, God will see to it that someone shows you the same welcome sometime in the future."

Amse elaborates: "It will be a reward to you or your family. Traditionally, a Senegalese mother welcomes guests into her house so that her children will be well received by others on their journeys."

I wave good-bye to them from the back of the taxi. As I settle back into my seat, the driver turns to me and begins a familiar dialogue. "Where are you from?" he asks.

"The United States."

"Are you married?"

"No."

"Do you have a Senegalese boyfriend?"

LESSON 2

Ndank ndank mooy japp golo ci ñaay
Step by step, you catch
the monkey in the jungle
Wolof Proverb

Like a hunter in the jungle with his eyes fixed
on his prey, up in the thick canopy of tangled branches,
we knew what we wanted and could only move towards
it one step at a time. Living in Senegal, where time is
measured by relationships built rather than minutes
passed, patience is the only way to stay the course.
From the beginning, our eyes were focused
on a clear target: a sustainable project that would
increase access to education in Senegal.

CHAPTER 4

Just on Time

I am slowing down. This I know because the walk to school that once took me five minutes now stretches itself over fifteen. My walk to the *Centre Baobab* is simple: from my new apartment I follow the main drag back towards Mami Chou's house, walk to the end of Mami Chou's block, turn right and walk down another residential block until I reach *Mosque de Karack*. From there, I walk about 500 meters on the dusty sidewalk, past small boutiques, women hunched over baskets of shriveled garden vegetables for sale, and *le couchonerie*, a butcher shop with pork hocks hanging from the ceiling and hungry patrons gnawing at juicy sandwiches.

Each morning, the first people I say hello to are my next-door neighbors—furniture builders who are outside by the time I leave each morning, working with their hands to shape raw timber into something useful, with only the aid of handsaw, sand paper, or wood planer. I used to say hello to them en groupe until I began to learn their names. Now I go through the whole spiel with each one individually.

Greeting someone in Senegal is a far cry from the American what's up? in passing. There is a very specific dialogue that you must go through, and it can easily take a few minutes each time. My morning dialogue with the neighbor goes something like this:

"*Assalam alaikum,*" I begin. Peace onto you.

"*Wa alaikum assalam,*" he responds. And peace back to you.

"*Nga def?*" I ask. How are you?

"*Maangi fii rekk,*" he responds. I am here, only.

"*Am nga jamm?*" I ask. Do you have peace?

"*Jamm rekk,*" he responds. Peace only.

"*Ana wah ker ga?*" I ask. How are the people of your house (your family)?

"*Noongi feu,*" he responds. They are there.

"*Nu ngeen jamm?*" I ask. Do they have peace?

"*Jamm rekk,*" he responds. Peace only.

"*Ana sa yaay?*" I ask. How is your mother?

"*Jamm rekk,*" he responds. Peace only.

"*Ana sa papa?*" I ask. How is your father?

"*Jamm rekk,*" he responds. Peace only.

"*Alhamdoolilay!*" I say. Praise God.

"*Alhamdoolilay!*" he says back. Praise God.

The better you know someone, the longer it takes because it is polite to ask about all the family members you know by name. Of course, it is only polite for them to ask you how everyone in your family is, again by name. Before the constant, daily repetition built my confidence to get through the dialogue, I held my breath until the first time I heard the word *rekk,* knowing once we got to that point I could answer *jamm rekk* to any of the questions without revealing my incomprehension.

While Wolof is the most commonly spoken language, and also the name of the largest ethnic group in Senegal, there are dozens of different ethnic groups who each have their own language (e.g., Serer, Joola, Pulaar). If you meet someone who does not share your first language, the two of you muddle through until you find common ground. This is only possible because the Senegalese are brilliant linguists, most of them speaking a minimum of three or four languages in order to effectively communicate with their neighbors.

Now that I've begun to know my neighbors, my walk to school takes more time. At the first corner, there is always a group of kids milling around, playing in the street. Sometimes, an older sister is sitting with her younger sister between her knees, braiding her hair, and I stop to say how pretty she looks. I leave to head down the short block to *Mosque de Karak*, watching out for potholes and, on occasion, flooding from broken sewer pipes.

There are several small boutiques set up on the final stretch to school, forcing me to weave my way through various vendors. The only permanent structure is a small wooden booth with enough room for one person inside, surrounded by walls of shelves filled with school supplies.

The other vendors are three to five women who come to the same spot each morning with baskets full of either *bissap* (hibiscus) leaves or the chalky white fruit of the baobab tree, both ingredients for fresh fruit juice. They sit on cement bricks or small wooden stools with their baskets displayed in front of them. Each morning, their chatter stops when I pass.

"*Toubab—begg nga bissap?*" one asks as the others look on. Their marketing strategy confounds me: how can they hope to make any money when they are all selling the same thing? I choose a different vendor among them each time I buy something, to spread the wealth.

On the other side of the main street, there is a paved sidewalk outside the mosque. Over there, I weave between men kneeling on prayer mats, either reading the Koran or waiting for the next call to prayer. At the end of the row of the devout, there is a produce seller, whose stand is double the size of the school supply seller. His staples are onions, potatoes, garlic, and bananas. Depending on the season I may get mango or guava or jackfruit there too. I stop at his stand often and can never leave without a few minutes of chit-chat.

As I become friendlier with the people in my neighborhood, my five-minute walk to school stretches out to fifteen or twenty minutes. Each day, I arrive to Zator's class later than the previous day. I usually find him sitting in his chair, his unlit pipe in his mouth, staring off into space.

"Katie," he says, turning to look at me sneak in. "Just on time."

CHAPTER 5

Ndank, Ndank

I am walking up the long dirt road that exits the Université Chiekh Anta Diop campus and meets the main street, a busy thoroughfare to downtown Dakar. Two hundred meters ahead in the distance are the student dormitories, usually bustling with people, but today eerily deserted. Lined up against the fence on my right are pushcarts piled high with books, notebooks, and other school supplies. One cart is dedicated exclusively to pens: either stacked in blue and black pyramids or hanging from the top of the cart in packages of three. The vendors give me a half-hearted sales pitch.

"*Toubab, veulliez-vous acheter les cahiers pour vos études?*" Do you want to buy notebooks for your studies?

I would buy notebooks, if I had confidence that my economics classes would start any time soon. I have been waiting nearly three months. In the meantime, I have been attending what I've come to call *French for Foreigners* classes at the University.

My classmates represent countries as diverse as Japan, Morocco, Russia, and Guinea. For all of us, French is our second or third language, keeping our conversations basic and time-consuming. Not a problem, given the time we spend waiting. Today, we waited for forty minutes for the teacher, and five minutes after he arrived, he excused himself to take a cell phone call, never returning. The first few times this happened, I turned to my neighbor and started chatting. Today, I just packed up my bag and left, wondering why I bothered to come at all.

I pass the last of the school supply merchants and see a young woman hurrying down the road towards me, holding a scarf over her mouth and nose. Beyond her I see a group of students standing in a line, their arms around their neighbors or their fists raised in the air. As I get closer, my nostrils start to burn. I cover my mouth and nose with the collar of my shirt.

I get to the wall of students and see why they are stopped. Fifty meters ahead of us, there is a team of police officers hoisting canisters of tear gas over the fence into the yard of the student dormitory. There, on the receiving end, is a group of six male students launching stones and bricks at the officers. All of this is happening in the center of a semicircle of spectators.

Sirens growing louder announce the arrival of a police van. It jumps the curb onto the dusty walkway, nearly plowing over the people who are now standing in its wake, covered in dust. I don't know whether to feel relieved or fearful.

The van spits officers out of its side door and they run to form a line near the fence of the dorms. Soon, they are launching more tear gas and it becomes difficult to breathe. My only exit is the narrow path behind the police officers. I am frozen with fear.

* * *

I chose to study at the University of Cheikh Anta Diop with my Rotary Ambassadorial Scholarship because it fit all my criteria: it was in French-speaking West Africa, had an economics program, and had a research institution that focused on human rights. Its only imperfection, revealed to me long after my decision, is that classes may not actually start.

A few weeks after our arrival in Dakar, I came to the University with Natalie Domond, another Rotary Ambassadorial Scholar, to register for classes. Natalie and I have become friends in our French and Wolof classes with Zator at the *Centre Baobab*, but we met months before leaving the United States, thanks to

Natalie's outreach. She took my phone number off the list of other students going to Senegal provided by Rotary and just called me up, out of the blue. As we prepared for our trip, we shared stories from our experiences at the required orientations, compared packing lists, and commiserated about the painfully slow process of getting a student visa.

"I don't get it," I told her over the phone one night when Senegal was still a place I'd never been. "When I called the Embassy and told the woman how ridiculous it was that she lost my paperwork, she asked me not to personally attack her. She said it would be a lot easier if we were friendly to one another." This was my first glimpse of the commitment of the Senegalese to conducting business only under the most amicable of circumstances.

Natalie did not stop with my name on that list, but contacted every other person listed. She is the type of person who responds to every one of your stories with "I know someone you should talk to." She is the one who met Babacar, a new friend familiar with the University, who accompanied us.

As we walked onto campus, I saw large empty buildings and the green space between them overgrown with wild grass and weeds. As Babacar led us to the bursar's office, I didn't see any other students.

"*Non, non, non, Mademoiselle. Je suis desolé,*" said the university employee, peering through stacks of paper at me. He was sorry, but he simply could not register me for classes. A thin man with round glasses and a white oxford shirt buttoned all the way to the neck, he reminded me of a boy playing dress up. He sat dwarfed behind a monstrous green, metal desk that filled the cramped room. On all four corners of the desk were stacks of papers, two feet high. The piles were of manila forms, filled out by hand, and stapled in groups. Behind the desk were two filing cabinets in the same army-green metal. The top drawer of one was wedged open and a bunch of forms fanned out like an accordion. On top of both of the file cabinets were stacks of paper that nearly reached the ceiling.

When my eyes reached the top, I was surprised to see a small ceiling fan circulating slowly. The room was hot and I felt no breeze whatsoever. It smelled like the library of my muggy elementary school, old paper cooking in the heat.

"*Mais, pourquoi?*" Why not, I asked him. I had my two required visa pictures, my acceptance letter from Professor Sene, whom I had never met but who penned the letter for me as a favor to a mutual friend, and my tuition for the year in cash. My pants pocket was bulging with a thick stack of bright purple 10,000 CFA bills worth $300.

"*Carte d'identie, oui. Mais registration, non.*" Both he and Babacar looked at Natalie and me expectantly. They could issue our student ID cards, but not register us for classes.

"*Mais, pourqoui?*" But why, I whined.

The seated man looked at me over the rims of his lenses and for a moment I had hope. Only in Senegal a few weeks, I already knew that the Senegalese will do almost anything to help someone out. The bureaucrat began to talk to Babacar in Wolof as I looked around. Despite the looming mountains of paper, the work area of his desk was clean, save for a few sugary rings from teacups.

"*Waaw, waaw,*" I heard Babacar say in agreement. He was nodding his head, listening intently. They spoke privately, with Natalie and me right there in front of them, for several minutes. When they stopped, Babacar turned to us.

"You can get your identity card and pay your tuition. He will also let you fill out the first registration form, but you cannot officially register today. He is sorry, there is nothing he can do." Seven minutes of dialogue translated in two sentences.

"*Est-ce qu'il a dit pourquoi?*" I asked why not in French, knowing the bureaucrat would understand.

The man in the buttoned up collared shirt laughed before responding.

"*Mademoiselle, c'est pas le bonne moment.*" It is not time.

This was my first glimpse of Senegalese time. Time moves in

Senegal, but quite differently than it does back home.

He opened his top desk drawer and handed us each a form.

"Fill this out and bring it back as soon as you can," he said. "Go down the hall for student identity cards. Don't forget to come back and say good-bye," he insisted.

Down the hall, in another plain room with army-green metal furniture, a woman dressed in a loose bright orange *booboo* gave us each a simple form to fill out. When we handed the forms back to her, she recopied all the information, by hand, onto a piece of printed yellow cardstock, folded it in half, dragged her long thumbnail down the crease, and then stapled our photographs inside. With a rubber stamp, she tapped a red ink pad and then the inside of the card. After signing the stamp, she leaned over and handed it to the woman sitting at the desk next to her. The second woman opened our cards, stamped them, signed the stamps, and then handed our student identity cards back to us.

"*Voila*," she said, smiling.

Babacar was a friend of Professor Sene, and assured us that it was best if we just gave him our tuition directly. He could bring it to his friends in the bursar's office and get us receipts to provide Rotary to prove that we paid for and, in theory, enrolled in university classes.

"We'll come back another day to see him," said Babacar. On our way out, we kept our promise to say good-bye to the original bureaucrat and knocked on his door to hand him the forms we filled out.

"Wow, you've already completed them," he said, seemingly surprised by our promptness. "We'll see you next time," he said as he stood up to shake our hands.

Natalie and Babacar walked out of the small room ahead of me and as I turned to say a final good-bye, I saw the man glance at our forms and then put them on the top of the stack in the front right corner of his desk.

While we waited for news about university classes, Natalie and

I extended our French and Wolof classes at the *Centre Baobab* with Zator.

The *Centre Baobab* serves a wide range of students: undergraduates, NGO employees, individual travelers, missionaries, professional expatriates, and Rotary and Fulbright scholars. An unassuming building from the outside, its friendly atmosphere engulfs you the moment you walk inside.

The classrooms are built around a central courtyard with white plastic tables and chairs under the shade of rainbow umbrellas, something that strikes me as a display at Home Depot. There are potted plants and palm fronds growing in the thin strip of soil around the edge of the courtyard, and three full-grown trees offer shade. A water jug with filtered water gives students the option to make tea or instant coffee. Throughout the day, during their breaks in classes, students and teachers mingle in the courtyard.

One afternoon during the break in Wolof class, Natalie and I sat in the courtyard wondering out loud what we would do if we couldn't register for classes. When would they start and how were we supposed to fulfill our scholarship requirements in the meantime?

Zator was smoking his pipe at the table next to ours and tried to reassure us.

"You are going to take classes," he said. "*Ndank, ndank.*"

"*Ndank, ndank?*" I asked. It didn't seem fair to introduce new material outside of the classroom. "What does that mean?"

Zator pulled in a long draw on his pipe and crossed one arm over his chest. He leaned back in his chair. With a man as old and wise as Zator, a simple translation was never sufficient.

"Katie, Natalie." Holding the bowl of his pipe, he looked at us. "When we get back into class, we will discuss the idea of time."

"What do you Americans say about time?" Zator asked, back in the classroom.

"There's no time like the present?" suggested Natalie.

Zator looked at us, smirking.

"*Vas-y*," he urged me on.

"Time flies when you're having fun," I said.

"Think of the way you talk about time," he said. "You spend time. You waste time. You run out of time. You never have enough time. You cannot find the time to do what you want.

"Time is money," he continued. "Isn't that the American mantra?"

"Time is not money," he said. "Time is not a thing. Time is nothing but an illusion. The Senegalese understand this. Rather than try to hold on to time, we hold on to our friends and family.

"Our ancestors have passed us the secret to accomplishing anything you want in due time." I dug around in my bag for a pen; this would be worth taking notes.

"*Ndank, ndank,*" He said. "*Ndank, ndank mooy japp golo ci nâay.*" He paused, expectantly. Neither Natalie nor I attempted to repeat that back to him.

"Step by step you will catch the monkey in the jungle," he smiled.

After several attempts to repeat the phrase, I gave up with a loud groan.

"Katie," Zator said. "*Ndank, ndank.* A seed planted today does not blossom tomorrow. You can only get where you want to go one step at a time. Step by step.

"Remember this when you become frustrated with your French and Wolof. You cannot learn a language all at once; you must learn it word by word. Step by step. *Ndank ndank.*"

To prove his point, he made us repeat the phrase back to him, word by word, until we had it memorized.

* * *

The next month passed, day by day, step by step, and I felt no closer to starting classes. It wasn't until December that we heard rumors on the radio that university registration had begun and while I was skeptical, curiosity brought me down to campus today.

As I look at the narrow space between the police officers and the fence on their left, I hear Zator's words. *Ndank, ndank.* Step by step may be an axiom of patience and prudence, but at this moment, it is what I need to muster up the wherewithal to put one foot in front of the other and step, quickly, out of the middle of chaos. I arrive safely on the other side, a few steps closer to the monkey in the jungle.

CHAPTER 6

Hurry Up and Wait

In the back of a taxi, I nervously tap my foot, looking out the window at the unmoving traffic. I have only three days for my weekend trip and want to make the most of it. Students at the *Centre Baobab* have shared horror stories of bus rides that took an entire day because the bus left Dakar so late. Although I am generally skeptical of our collective high expectations as Americans, I could not find a Senegalese person to assuage my fears.

"Arrive as early as you can, you want to be there when the bus leaves," was the most definitive bus schedule I could get from anyone.

As my taxi pulls into the Colabane bus station, a handful of young men my age, loitering around the entrance, see me in the back seat and start running alongside my cab. I know their gig: they are opportunist entrepreneurs who offer their guidance through the bus station maze for a fee.

"Where are you going, Madame?" they ask breathlessly through the window. "Saint Louis? Fatick? Thiès?"

From the guidebooks and guidance of friends, I understand the various options for travel: a private taxi, which is exorbitantly expensive. The *sept-place*, a station wagon with room for seven. A mid-size van which seats about thirteen. Or the *Ndigendiaye*, a large bus that seats thirty. The price goes down as the seating capacity increases. A student waiting for classes to start, rich in time and poor in money, I choose the *Ndigendiaye*.

I insist to the taxi driver that he take me all the way to the bus. Getting out early only gives the guide the opportunity to accompany me and then demand I pay him for his service.

We drive through the narrow passage left between buses, taxis, and cars parked side by side. When the taxi can go no farther and stops at the end of a pedestrian walkway, I pay the driver and clutch my purse tightly to my chest before exiting the cab. Made clumsy by my large backpack, I lumber through hundreds of travelers, merchants, porters, transients, beggars, and drivers. We are all sandwiched in the narrow space between bumpers of parked buses. In front of each bus, the porters squawk their destination cities, trying with the volume and frequency of their calls to persuade the ambivalent wanderers.

"FIMELA!" says a bug-eyed man dressed in all black. "Fimela. Fimela. Fimela." Spotting me, "*Toubab*-Fimela?"

I bargain a fair price for stowing my backpack, the equivalent of checked baggage, on the roof of the bus. I climb in the bus through the rear door and feel lucky to be the second person aboard. With all the seats open, I have my choice. Without hesitation, I settle into a window seat near the front.

The seat is tattered vinyl, stretched tightly over plywood, with no cushion. There is space for two people on my bench and, on the other side of the narrow aisle, another identical bench. Between the two, there is a wooden plank that folds down to make a fifth seat. The unfortunate person sitting there will sit the entire ride without any back support.

Over the next half hour, other passengers trickle in. Still unsure what time the bus leaves, I feel hopeful when eight passengers arrive at once. Maybe we are getting close to departure time.

"Excuse me," I ask the man sitting next to me. "When does the bus leave?"

He glances around the empty bus behind us.

"There are about twenty seats left," he says. "As soon as they are full."

It takes me a minute to realize what he is saying. Like Zator said in class, the time of departure depends on people, not minutes.

"I hope we leave before lunch," I say.

"*Inshallah*," he says. In Arabic, God willing. A phrase used daily to punctuate the idea that the ultimate control of our lives rests in the hands of a greater power.

It gets hotter in the bus as the late morning sun rises to afternoon, but I wait in my seat because I see no relief outside. From my window, I count eighteen buses and four times as many people in my direct line of sight. People waiting. People buying. People selling. Down one row of buses, indifferent to the sensibilities of observers, one man crouches down and takes a piss.

To pass the time, I take out my journal and write a list of all the things that vendors are dangling in front of my window.

Girls' patent leather shoes. Hardboiled eggs with chili powder. Homemade hibiscus popsicles. Razors. Sunglasses. Cell phone holders. Plastic toy cell phones with videogame-like rings. Kola nuts. Toothpaste. The neatly carved branches of the neem tree, the poor farmer's toothbrush. Q-tips. Batteries. The Koran and religious pamphlets written in Arabic. Ginger root. Teakettles. Cigarettes. Batik dresses. Shuttlecocks. Red lace thongs. Underwire bras. Alarm clocks. Bananas. Mangoes. Bread. Fried dough.

The man next to me buys some hot rolls, leaning across my lap to pass his money through the open window. When he offers me a roll, my hunger accepts before my politesse can refuse. I have been sitting in the bus for hours and haven't eaten since breakfast. He offers one to the guy seated in front of us, who has decided to balance a full duffel bag on his lap rather than paying to put it up top. Two seats in front of me, a woman is nursing her tiny baby, who is hidden under the colorful fabric draped over the mother and child.

Because it is December, a month of celebration, many of the travelers are bringing home food for a good family dinner. I watch as the porter lifts three live goats and ties them to the rooftop of the bus. A few minutes later, a stream of yellow urine trickles down the window of the seat next to the nursing mother. Her hands occupied, she asks the man next to her in a panic to shut the window. Two chickens have been tied to the seat posts in the back of the bus, their squawking and wings beating against the floor adding to the noise of a nearly-full bus. I see only one seat empty.

Forty minutes later, that same seat is still empty.

"Driver," shouts a man from the back of the bus. "Let's go! The bus is full." Other passengers agree in chorus. The driver shouts back but makes no move.

Finally, an old woman boards the bus, taking the one available seat above the chickens, and the engine roars and spits and sputters. We wait fifteen minutes while the porter finds the chauffer of the bus parked in front of us and gets him to move it. Nearly three hours after I've arrived, we leave our parking spot and head out of the bus stop.

I turn to the man seated next to me.

"Any idea what time we will arrive?" I ask.

"When our trip is over," he responds. *"Inshallah."*

LESSON 3

Nit, nit ay garabam
Man is man's best remedy
Wolof Proverb

Just as anything worth having is worth sharing in Senegal, anything worth doing is worth doing together. Project Japalé Gouné was not built by Ling Ling, Natalie, and me, but by the people we were lucky enough to meet along the way: friends and family, staff at the school, Rotarians around the world.

CHAPTER 7

My Cousin, the Fat Pig

S tretching my legs after the cramped bus ride from Dakar, I wait for the porter to throw my backpack down from the roof. I am in the small village of Samba Dia on my way to the Sine Saloum Delta. Taking advantage of the delay in classes start-ing, I am in search of ripe mangoes, lush mangroves, or anything else that will help me forget how far I am from my family back home in Wisconsin on a weekend I feel particularly homesick.

I look around the village bus depot, a vast, dusty field lined with small boutiques and filled with groups of juice sellers waiting for the next arrival. I see immediately that today is a lucky day: I have arrived on the one day of the week that the bus stop trans-forms into a busy market.

In search of a snack for my next ride, I stroll up and down aisles of vendors who are squatting next to their goods. Faded second-hand T-shirts folded in piles three feet high. Bunches of bananas reaching from the vendor's mat like a hand with dozens of edible yellow fingers. Multicolored plastic buckets and teakettles. Sticky pyramids of red and green mangoes, their leaking nectar glisten-ing in the afternoon sun.

Finally, I find what I am looking for—an old woman sitting on an overturned wooden crate displaying peanuts for sale. She has forty plastic bags, each holding a handful of either plain or sugar-coated peanuts. Her head is wrapped in a fluorescent pink piece of fabric, folded like a crown. Gray hair peeks out at her temples. She is chewing on a *neem* branch, a favorite toothbrush of many rural

Senegalese. When we start to talk, she does not take out the branch but, rather, pushes it to the corner of her mouth, where it bounces with her every word.

I greet her in Wolof, eager to practice. Three days of navigating from one small town to the next have improved my language more than months of classroom lessons. I launch into the customary greeting, ask about her family, ask if she feels at peace, and then we both praise God. Eventually, I get around to asking her how much the peanuts cost.

My Wolof is not native enough to avoid getting quoted the *toubab*, or foreigner, price. I decided to bargain her down in Senegalese style: taking my time with friendly small talk.

She asks my Senegalese name.

"Kumba N'dour." I reply. By sharing my adopted last name, I am revealing that I belong to the Serer, one of the dozens of ethnic groups in Senegal. I know that if she is also Serer, I will have no problem negotiating. The Senegalese believe in solidarity.

"What a terrible name," she says, with a straight face. "You must be very stupid."

Without flinching, I ask her name.

"N'daiye Diatta."

Her last name tells me that she is Joola, another of the tribes. In fact, the Joola are considered cousins of the Serer.

I look her straight in the eye. "Joola?" I ask, raising an eyebrow. "You are selfish and love to eat rice, you pig."

The two vendors on either side of her have been listening with mostly disinterest until this point. At that moment, they burst out laughing, repeating what I have said.

"Kumba N'dour. *Begg na cebb.*" One of the women slaps her knee as she laughs.

Other vendors on the periphery hear and stroll over to check out the commotion. As I try to reassure myself I have said the right word for pig, my hands grow clammy and I become aware of the circle of strangers closing in around me.

The peanut vendor has not smiled once. She still looks stone cold, the neem stick dangling out of the corner of her mouth.

"*Begg na cebb?*" she asks. "I like rice? I don't think so. You," she says, pointing at me. "You are my slave and I know you spend all day eating peanuts." At this point the growing crowd around me erupts in laughter. The woman smiles, and with relief, I start laughing too.

As members of cousin ethnic groups, the Joola and Serer, we are "joking cousins." This means that when we meet, as a sign of friendliness, we insult each other without hesitation. Every ethnic group in Senegal has at least one or two joking cousin groups, so meeting one is rare enough to be a delight but common enough that the teasing and insults are protocol.

Once everyone surrounding us settles down, she sells me the peanuts for half the original asking price.

"Kumba N'dour," she says. "Come eat dinner with my family tonight."

I thank her and say I will next time. As I settle into my bus seat and wave good-bye, I feel like I am not so far from family this weekend after all.

CHAPTER 8

Homesick

One of the essential steps in preparing for my trip to Senegal was to immunize myself against the diseases of West Africa. My doctor had prescribed Mefloquine pills for malaria, booster shots for my Measles, Mumps & Rubella vaccine, immunizations against three strands of hepatitis, and emergency antibiotics strong enough to knock out giardia, ecoli, or any other bug invading my gastrointestinal tract. There was nothing, however, that I could take to protect myself from the ailment that has me feeling depressed, alone, unmotivated, and regretting my decision to come to Senegal. Homesickness.

If you are lucky enough to survive homesickness once, it lies dormant deep within you, like malaria, and can resurface at any time. My first case was at Mami Chou's house, when I was totally overwhelmed with the constant company of others. Now, I have settled into my own apartment and the malady has resurfaced.

I never intended to stay at Mami Chou's for more than a month; the family-stay was a required component of my first month of intensive French and Wolof classes, and it did wonders for my language. At the same time, the introvert in me struggled to get the alone time I needed to reenergize each day. The studio apartment that I rent is only a ten-minute walk away from Mami Chou's. She made me promise to come back and visit, which I do frequently, especially now that I am so homesick.

During the week, my Wolof classes keep me distracted and tire me out enough for a good night's sleep. The weekends, however, with all the time in the day to myself, I start to feel the melancholy creeping back in. The heaviness that keeps me lying in my bed, wide-awake at all hours; the saturated tear ducts, ready to leak at a moment's notice; the aching chest, my heart swollen with longing for home. The only thing more compelling than staring at the ceiling and wondering why I came to Senegal—the only thing that will actually get me out of bed—is a trip to *le cyber*.

Le cyber, or cyber café, is the place in my neighborhood for young people to see and be seen, both in person and online. Built in the lower level of a residential home down the street from Mami Chou's house, *le cyber* is a small office attached to a large square room with tables on the periphery, holding rows of computers. For a few hundred CFA, you can get online for an hour. Depending on the time of day, the sounds of *le cyber* shift. In the afternoon, when school gets out, squealing adolescents and giggling teenagers fill the room, chatting online with their friends, most of whom are likely seated three chairs down from them. The posted sign that reads, "One Chair Per Computer" does not deter kids from pooling their money for a shared hour of Internet access. The most savvy sits on the chair and controls the mouse, while another perches on the leader's lap, and a third stands behind them, draping his or her arms casually over the other two, bending forward to read the monitor.

In the early evening, while children are at home helping prepare dinner, *le cyber* is empty except for the American students, whose English dominates, usually through celebrity news or other headlines shouted across the room. Late at night, after dinner and until the midnight closing hour, the twenty-somethings, both Senegalese and American, saunter in. The din of conversation is overpowered by the popular hip-hop music emanating from the speakers of most computers. On a good night, the music is loud enough to mask the amorous sounds of passion from porn sites favored by the few clientele sitting in the darkest corner of the room.

Le cyber is the place to run into a friend, either in the flesh or in the virtual world. When I miss home as much as I do this Saturday evening, I go there to spend hours writing long emails to friends and family. My first drafts are riddled with typos and misplaced punctuation because of the French keyboard, and it is a luxury to take all the time I need to write a flawless letter.

The emails from my friends are always bittersweet. Like me, they are in the thick of their early-twenties, a time when a personal search for purpose can consume you entirely. For those not afflicted by such introspection, it is an ideal time to take your youthful beauty and tolerance for sleep deprivation out for a night on the town—every night and with a constantly evolving group of friends.

"My weekend was spent dancing and drinking Guiness with frat guys from Harvard," a friend back in Boston writes. *"This probably sounds trite to someone who is busy saving the world."* Trite? It actually sounds pretty appealing to someone who is trying mostly to save herself from herself. One must get out of bed, and ideally with a purpose, to make positive change in the world.

When all my responses are written and all my live chats are concluded, I still feel unwilling to disconnect. I read the New York Times and Milwaukee Journal Sentinel online, my appetite for news from home insatiable. Then comes the moment when my prepaid time runs out and the screen in front of me goes blank.

My heart sinks. I sit motionless for a moment, trying to prepare for reentry into le cyber, then my neigborhood, Karak, and ultimately my daily life here. I gather my wits, then my purse, and leave le cyber for home.

Outside there is a small group gathered around the beignet seller, a woman who sells fried doughballs sprinkled with sugar for 10 CFA each. A greasy indulgence that smells a lot like the food sellers at the Wisconsin State Fair. Enough change jangles in my pocket for at least five beignets. I stand in line and wait.

"Hello, Katie," says the woman. She is as round and plump as the doughballs she sells. "How are you?"

"Good, thanks," I respond. "And you?" I watch her scoop spoonfuls of gooey batter into a vat of boiling oil, where the batter sizzles and solidifies into round balls. She waits for them to fry crispy and then scoops them out with a slotted spoon into a metal bowl of sugar. She sprinkles them with more sugar, wraps them up in a paper cone made from yesterday's newspaper, and hands them over to me. When I grab them, the oil has already leaked through the newspaper, making my hands greasy.

"Katie?" says the young man standing next to me. "How are you?" He speaks in English, which surprises me. I turn to him and see a man slightly older than I, dressed in a colorful patchwork tunic, and wearing a string of wooden beads around his neck.

"Katie, hello," he says. "I am Ibu. Do you remember me?"

"Of course, Ibu. How are you?" I am certain that I have never met Ibu before, but know better than to insult him by saying so. As with so many social situations in Senegal, a little white lie that keeps people united is preferable to the truth that separates them.

Around Ibu's neck, hung on the string of beads, is a small frame with the photo of a man in a white headscarf. Ibu's long hair is in dreadlocks, many of them decorated with cowrie shells and colorful glass beads. Around his wrists, ankles, and upper arms he wears several visible *gris gris*, or protective amulets made from leather, twine, and other natural fibers. His distinct style of dress is that of a Baye Fall, a kind of Rastafarian disciple to a holy man named Ibra Fall.

"Your English is good, Ibu," I say.

"Oh, I don't speak English," he says. "I just know small words."

"Well, I'd be happy to speak Wolof half as well as you speak English," I say as I turn to walk home.

"May I walk with you?" he asks. "I am going in the same direction." Rather than question how he knows which direction I am headed, I shrug my shoulders and nod in the direction I am walking. Like so many other times in Senegal, taking the company of a relatively unfamiliar man to fend off the attention of complete male strangers whom I may encounter feels safer than walking alone.

"How is your family?" he asks, again in English.

"Good," I say. "I just got an email from my parents and they are doing well."

"All right," he says. "Do you feel peace?"

I am taken aback hearing the question in my own language. I have been asked *am nga jamm* hundreds of times in Wolof, but this is the first time someone has asked me in English.

"I, uh, yes..." I stall, searching for the right words to respond. "Nothing but peace." I notice, also for the first time in answering this question, that my body relaxes as I say it. My muscles must still be trained only in English.

As we walk, I offer Ibu my beignets, still hot to the touch. He takes one without hesitation and pops it in his mouth.

"Katie," Ibu says. "You look tired. Have you been sick?"

"Kind of," I reply. "In a way."

"*Nit nit ay garabam,*" Ibu says, still smiling.

"What does that mean?" I ask.

"Man is man's best remedy," he says. "It's a proverb that reminds us the best way to heal is to spend time with other people."

"Well, then. You arrived right on time," I say. After a lull in the conversation, I ask Ibu what he did today.

"The sun is shining, the weather is hot," he says. "I am enjoying."

I chuckle. It is out of habit that I still ask people what they did, were doing, or plan to do that day. It is a completely foreign question to the Senegalese. It is as out of place as them asking me if I have peace, in English.

In fact, in the months I have lived in Senegal, not one single Senegalese person has yet asked me America's favorite get-to-know-you question: "What do you do?" They don't care. They are much more concerned about the well-being of my family.

"Where did you learn English, Ibu?" I ask. "Did you take classes at the University?"

His eyes bug out with surprise and he clutches the framed picture hanging on his neck.

"The University! I am higher man," he laughs and lifts the frame towards the sky. "But I no higher education man."

"Well, then," I ask. "Who taught you?"

"Bob." He smiles contently at me, his expression returning to its relaxed state.

"Bob?" I ask.

"Bob Marley," he says, matter-of-factly.

I should have known. I have yet to meet a Senegalese man between the ages of 13 and 60 who doesn't love Bob Marley. I hear his reggae music blasted from market shops, shortwave hand-held radios, and taxis every day. People hum and sing along, most of them without understanding a single word.

"Every time I hear Bob Marley songs, I feel happy and want comprehension." He taps his pointer finger on his temple. "So I write the words in my mind and find a friend who speak English."

"How do you remember all those words?" I ask, shocked. "Do you keep a notebook or something?"

"Only written in head and heart. Not on paper," he says. In my mind, I see the post-it notes stuck to inanimate objects in my apartment, their Wolof names scribbled on the yellow squares, my mute Wolof tutor. Writing a language and speaking a language do not necessarily come as a package.

As we turn onto my street, I lead Ibu one block past my apartment, as I do with all the other male suitors who have offered, at one time or another, to walk me home.

"Here we are," I lie. "My apartment," and I gesture vaguely to several houses behind me.

"Okay, Katie," he says. "Tomorrow, or after tomorrow, you come my house, drink *attayah*." An offer to come drink Senegalese tea.

"Yes," I say. "I will come soon." I turn down an alley that leads away from my apartment and watch Ibu walk away. When he is out of sight, I duck back onto the street and walk back to my apartment.

My homesick insomnia is stronger than the dose of company that Ibu provided. Just as I am about to start recording my misery in my journal, the lights in my apartment go out. Such neighborhood-wide power cuts are frequent, almost daily, so I've grown accustomed to them and have gathered an arsenal of candles.

I opt not to risk burning the pages of my journal with dripping candle wax. Putting my journal away, I cook an omlette for dinner on my two-burner gas countertop stove. I settle into bed to watch the *Virgin Suicides* DVD, rented from the local movie store, on my laptop. My computer's battery life should outlast the electricity cut.

I lie back, under my mosquito net with the lights off, and feel transported back home. Before me on the screen is a family of girls that look like me, talk like me, make me laugh. I can't understand why the characters are so sad; they are living in a house with their family and seeing their friends every day at school. It seems indulgent of them to feel depressed when there are people like me, living thousands of miles from home, and far away from anything familiar.

When the movie ends, I feel that same jarring feeling I had earlier at *le cyber* when familiar faces and headlines from my hometown newspaper were snatched from me. For a moment, I feel heavy with the realization that I am alone in a dark apartment in Senegal. Quickly, before I can think twice about it, I replay the movie, this time in French with English subtitles; might as well try to learn something while I feel like shit.

I fall asleep during the third film showing and dream of home. In the dream, my friends and I are all together in the big house from the movie. We are happy and laughing, and I understand all the jokes that people make. I can't see their faces, but it doesn't matter: context clues and body language are not nearly as important as understanding their spoken words. I reach out, trying to touch their faces, and I startle myself awake by tugging at my mosquito net. I roll over and see the sun coming up outside my apartment window; the only way to avoid dealing with my day is to sleep through it. I close my eyes and will myself back to dreamland.

When I finally do get out of bed, it is sometime between morning and night and I have a strong need to hear the voice of a friend, my best friend. I quickly throw on a wrinkled skirt and wrap my messy hair in a scarf. I walk to the telecenter, practically trotting with anticipation.

The telecenter is a small room off the side of le cyber with nothing more than four small phone booths against the far wall, each with a door. Nelson, the same guy who sells tickets for Internet usage, sells time on the phones for long distance calls.

"I'd like to call the United States," I say. Nelson looks me up and down and then nods to the booth.

"Go ahead," he says.

The booth is three square feet of sweltering heat. The small fan mounted in the upper corner is busted—that figures. I dial the country code and my best friend's number. Hearing her voicemail message chokes me up: I can't leave a message for fear that I'll start crying. I take a deep breath before leaving the booth.

"I've finished," I tell Nelson, handing over a big purple 10,000 CFA bill to pay my 350 CFA tab.

"Sorry, I don't have change," he says. "I'll give it to you next time."

"What do you mean? How can you not have change?" I will immerse myself into a new place, rolling with each cultural punch, until the moment I suspect someone's taking advantage of me. Then I can play the high-maintenance American with ease.

"You are paying with a 10,000 CFA bill," he says, waving the crisp, purple paper in his hand. "We do not have change for that."

"Well, what I am supposed to do?" I ask. "That's my money."

"I said, 'I'll give it to you tomorrow.' Come back and I may have change," he says.

"*May* have change?" Today is not the day to test my patience. "I am not going to leave all that money here. It is a lot of money. How can you not have change? What kind of business are you not to have change?" I am asking the same questions over and over again in my basic Wolof. *No change, why? Why no change? That's impossible, no change.* Even I am aware of how unreasonable, and slightly crazy, I sound repeating myself, but I am afraid if I stop I will start crying.

Nelson looks over at a friend sitting nearby, a silent observer until now. They talk briefly in Wolof and then the friend takes the 10,000 CFA bill and walks into the computer room.

"No problem. He will find change," Nelson says.

"See," I say smugly, "I knew you had change."

The tall friend stands at the doorway of the computer lab and whistles.

"Boy!" he says. A dozen brown heads with razor-cut black hair turn to look at him. He makes eye contact with a boy sharing a chair in the far corner. The boy gets up, hurries over, and stands in front of the tall guy, who gives instructions. The young boy says nothing, but nods obediently and then takes the bill and runs off. His flip-flop sandals smack the linoleum tile on his way out.

I am bewildered to see my money change hands three times in front of me, but I just don't have the energy to protest. I collapse in the chair vacated by the tall man and look at Nelson for guidance.

"The boy will get you change," he says. "Have a seat and wait." He looks me straight in the eye. "You must be new to Dakar," he says, "if you don't know about the change problem."

"The change problem?" I ask.

"Yes. Senegal is a poor country and money is difficult to find. It is not like America where George Bush prints more money every time he needs it." I laugh at the absurdity.

I make small talk with Nelson and his friend, who I learn is a student at the University. I ask him when he thinks classes will start.

"Anytime now," he says. "*Inshallah.*"

Nelson entertains us with stories of a busy weekend out dancing with friends and trying his luck with a few ladies at the club. As we talk, I am surprised by the sound of my own laughter. Could I actually be enjoying myself? When the little boy returns with a fistful of change, I get the same jarring feeling I had the day before when my happy place was taken from me abruptly.

The boy hands me a crumpled ball of bills. One of the 100 CFA bills, a small orange one, is so badly worn that it has been nearly laminated with scotch tape to keep it intact. The handful of coins he gives me is heavy and leaves a metallic smell on my palm.

"Don't go!" Nelson says when I get up to leave. "Sit. Stay. Talk." His offer is genuine but, like the movie and my emails, all good things must end. I'd rather feel like I have some control over when.

Walking home, I look down at my wrinkled skirt. I should do some laundry, but even sulking around my apartment feeling alone is more appealing then spending hours hand-washing all of my clothes in a plastic bucket on the porch. Still, I gravitate towards the boutique for laundry detergent because a girl has her limits.

"Katie!" a familiar voice says. "*Nga def?*" I look up to see Ibu leaving the boutique with two plastic bags: one of sugar and the other of black tea leaves. "You come my house for tea," he says.

The polite thing to do would be to refuse Ibu's offer at first; let him insist, even after a second refusal. Finally, after some time, I should accept with feigned resignation, a tribute to my friend that nothing, even previous plans, is more appealing than spending time with him. Today, with laundry as my alternative, I have no time for social nuance. I accept immediately.

He opens the gate to his house and leads me into a courtyard tiled in mosaics, where he invites me to sit in a chair set up in the shade of a banana tree growing in the urban garden. Several family members come outside to say hello and welcome me, each of them shaking my hand. They stick around until Ibu comes back;

it would be terribly rude to leave a houseguest all alone. Ibu shows up carrying a large red canister of gas and the wire frame of a burner. He puts them together and, just like that, we have a gas stove in front of us.

Set out on a metal plate is a bag of black tea leaves, a bag of white sugar, a small red teapot with a black, sooty bottom, and two small glasses only slightly larger than souvenir shot glasses. A plastic pitcher of water is at Ibu's feet.

He fills one of the glasses with tea leaves and dumps them into the pot. Then he fills each glass with water and dumps those into the pot, too. He puts the pot on the burner and ignites the gas.

I look at Ibu, dressed in the same patchwork tunic, with his long, ratty dreads framing his face. He stands out in this neighborhood of distinguished middle class men in well-pressed tunics or suit jackets. I don't know what, but something just doesn't fit.

"Ibu, tell me what it means to be a Baye Fall," I say.

"Baye is Father. Fall is Ibra Fall," he begins. "Fall is holy, holy man. Father of our people." He grabs the framed photo on his chain of beads and holds it up for me to see. He then lifts the teapot by the handle, twirls it in a slight circle to mix the tea leaves and water. The bitter scent of boiling black tea leaves wafts into the air.

"For Baye Falls, work is prayer. Fastest road to Allah is with holy man," he continues. "For Baye Fall, Ibra Fall is holy man."

"Allah?" I ask. "So you are also Muslim?"

"Yes."

"Do you go to the mosque?"

"No," he says. "We pray big group. Very music, very singing."

I actually heard this prayer ritual one Friday night while visiting Natalie. In the open soccer field in front of her house, a group of about thirty Baye Falls played drums, chanted, and danced for a few hours. The jovial atmosphere and wafting smell of marijuana made me assume the Baye Falls were a Friday night party crew.

Ibu lifts and rotates the teapot again, this time lifting the lid to look inside. A few minutes later, he fills one of the cups with sugar and dumps it into the teapot. He whisks it again, and the sweet smell of burnt sugar makes me salivate.

"To be honest, Ibu," I say, "I see the Baye Falls downtown, begging and smelling like cali smoke and I thought they were a party group. Certainly not a religion."

Ibu laughs and then is silent for a moment. "Okay," he says. "I see Americans on television: rich, fat, and afraid of Muslims. You all like that?" Point taken.

After the tea has been boiling for at least five minutes, he fills each of the cups with the dark liquid and then dumps their contents back into the teapot. He refills the cups, but lifts the teapot high above the glasses as he pours. The hot tea cascades into the cup with a frothy head. When he empties the tea back into the pot, he lifts the cup in the same way, letting the froth stick to the sides of the glasses. He repeats this—filling and emptying the teacups, each time lifting the teapot high as if he were drawing the tea out of the cup—until each of the glasses is full: half tea and half sugary froth.

He hands me a glass. It is sticky and burns my fingers. I watch Ibu put the metal teapot back on the gas burner with ease.

"Doesn't that burn your hands?" I ask.

He smiles and displays his palms for my benefit. They are thick with hard, calloused skin.

"I am a farmer boy," he says. "For Baye Fall, second road to Allah is work."

"How does a farm boy work in the city?" I ask.

"Work is very difficult to find in Dakar," he says. "I am lucky to have my uncle here." He points his hand over his shoulder to the house behind him. "Other Baye Falls in Dakar have to ask money to support Fall."

"You mean beg?" I ask.

"Beg?" He seems unfamiliar with the word. "Asking for help means beg?"

I take a small sip from the glass, but the tea is still too hot to drink. Ibu picks up his glass and drinks it with the loudest slurping sound I've ever heard. I can't help but giggle.

"Try it," he says. "It makes cold the tea."

With a bit of hesitation, I bring the small glass to my lips and slurp it shyly. It feels a bit cooler in my mouth, so I echo Ibu's loud slurping with the abandon of a child given permission to blow bubbles in her soda.

"My father grew up on a dairy farm," I say, attempting to hurdle across the expanse between our lives.

"Very good," Ibu says. "Cows give milk. Milk sells. Your father, rich man."

"What type of farm do you work on?" I ask, deciding to omit the fact that my father left the farm, never to return to its work, after high school. In my life, the farm only meant visits to grandma and her great scalloped potatoes. Our visits, never frequent enough, gave my sister and me the chance to feed cows, play hide and seek in the corn fields, and dare each other to brave the creepy root cellar. For the first time, thoughts of my family make me feel proud instead of heart-broken and lonely. Somehow, I know the time between now and when I see them again will pass too quickly.

"Peanuts," Ibu answers.

"Is it far from here?" I ask.

"Katie," he says, looking down into his teacup. "It is a lifetime away."

He gulps down the last bit of black tea in his cup and then washes out the remaining bits of tea leaves with water. He shakes his cup to dry, scattering droplets over the dusty courtyard, each one landing on the tile with the momentary power to magnify and brighten the image and color below it. In a matter of minutes, the Sahel's heat has stolen back each drop, leaving only silt and dust in its place.

I hand my tea glass back to Ibu and make the motions to leave. "Katie," Ibu says. "You stay for second and third, right?"

"What?" I asked, confused.

"We serve three rounds of tea," he said. "The first is bitter like death, the second is sweet like love, and the third is smooth and delicious like life. But you have to be patient enough to wait for it."

"*Ndank, ndank,*" I say. I hand over my cup and settle in for a long day of tea, feeling the best I have all week. Maybe Ibu is right: good company is the best cure around.

LESSON 4

Inshallah *Arabic*
Su sube yallah *Wolof*
God willing

Yalla , yalla bay sa toll
Call upon God, but first plant your field
Wolof Proverb

*Like the millet farmer who plants seeds in May and works
tirelessly every day for months without reward, we believed
we could one day reap the harvest of our hard work.
Surrendering the details of its manifestation to a higher
power, we expected nothing but our dream. "We are
limited only by our imagination," Ling Ling reminded us.*

CHAPTER 9

Inshallah

Traveling alone is an act of faith. A belief that around each corner you will find something good and worth your while. The faith that when you find yourself alone and helpless, someone who can help will find you. Belief that getting lost is not a waste of time. Faith that a higher power—destiny, Allah, karma, a *Lonely Planet* guidebook—is the only companion you need to guide you in the right direction.

When I jump out of the back of a share taxi on a dusty road in the middle of rural Senegal on Christmas day, I have faith that the road will lead me to Yayeme, a small Serer village with about eighty large farming families, that I have chosen as a stop out of my guidebook.

When I ask the gaunt man folded into the small bus seat next to me how much farther to the Yayeme stop, his eyes widen and his chin lowers, as if he is peering over an invisible pair of bifocals to get a good look at me. He says nothing but raps his fingers on the metal roof of the bus, the noise from his silver ring signaling the driver to stop.

"*Toubab* missed the Yayeme stop," he says in Wolof. "Let her out here."

I exit the back of the taxi and the porter hands me my backpack from the roof. As the bus revs up its engine again, ready to leave me standing in the middle of a nondescript sandy road, I point in the direction from which we came.

"This road goes to Yayeme?" I ask the passengers in the back of the bus.

"*Inshallah*," responds a man I cannot see. This does not give me any confidence.

Inshallah, Arabic for "God willing," is invoked after practically every statement, commitment, or plan of action: the Senegalese understand that God controls their destiny. Surrendering control over much of their lives to a higher power gives the Senegalese a collective optimism rooted in complete faith in God's goodwill. However, it has the annoying side effect of surrendering accountability. A friend stands you up and you cannot even blame her: it simply was in the Master's plan.

My faith in God's directions would waver less if the man in the bus had responded definitively with detailed landmarks I could look for along the way. I raise a hand to wave good-bye to the taxi, already ten yards down the road.

It is late afternoon and the sun is beating down, making the sand underfoot very hot. I am thirsty, hungry, and technically lost, but I haven't felt better in days: this is the first time I have been without company (either a self-appointed guide, suitor, or curious child) in days. I took advantage of a long break in classes to see rural Senegal and have been traveling south down the coast, stopping in small fishing villages along the way to Gambia, a neighboring country I got a visa to visit. I do not plan to stay anywhere more than one night until I get there. Yayeme is just another village I plan on sleeping in and leaving early in the morning. I take in a deep breath of the fresh country air and stand up straighter.

Everything I need for the next ten days is in an oversized backpack that is sticking to my sweaty back. As I walk down the sandy road, on either side of me are vast plots of land. It is the dry season (it's been four months since any rain) and the earth is hot and the vegetation brittle. Tall prairie grass grows to my right in rows, a sure sign that these fields were cultivated this season; most likely they were peanut fields. A millet field ahead of me reminds me of a cornfield in late autumn back home in Wisconsin, with stubby brown stalks, the remnants of once-tall plants. In the distance, I can see the occasional palm or baobab tree.

Gradually the fields turn into hay fences. Stems of tall dried grass held up between sticks outline the periphery of each family's yard. Peering through breaks in the first fence I approach, I see three huts, four cement walls holding up palm leaf roofs. One hundred feet from me, a shirtless woman is sitting on a mat in the shade of a mango tree. Like the gumdrop trees of my Candyland childhood, the branches above her are dotted with sweet orange fruits.

In one arm, she breastfeeds a baby wrapped in yellow and black print fabric. Her other hand is inside a *calabash*, a dried gourd the size of a beach ball, where she picks out stones from the rice she will prepare for dinner. Behind the cover of the fence where she doesn't see me, I search her face for signs of her age; she looks no older than I.

A small toddler seated next to her bangs his hands on an overturned calabash as if it were a bongo drum. Two boys, around age six, are doodling in the sand with sticks. The larger of the two draws his stick up like a weapon, and jabs it at the other, who returns in kind. Over the sounds of clashing wooden swords, the mother shouts a few stern words and they go back to tracing in the sand.

From the direction I am heading comes an underfed brown horse pulling a tall, thin man on a wooden cart. I say hello to the driver and count the horse's protruding ribs as they trot by. The mother and children look up to watch the traffic and see me.

"*Toubab! Toubab! Toubab!*" the boys shout. I have been spotted.

I walk over and ask the mother for directions to *Daam Sa Doole Campement*, the campsite/hostel listed in my *Lonely Planet Senegal* guidebook. She doesn't know, so she has her son, the elder of the sword fighters, lead me into town to find someone who can help me. He brings me to two men, Musa and Doodoo, who offer to walk me to the *campement*, or hostel campground. They tell me they are brothers and know everyone in the village.

"Diène, the guy who works there, is a good friend of ours," says Musa, the older of the two.

We reach a gate, constructed out of long sheets of tree bark, and Musa shouts over it.

"*Njape. Gere meke.*" I don't understand what he says, but I do understand that it isn't Wolof. This is a Serer village, and the mother tongue has changed.

The gate opens and a young man stands in the entrance. He wears a ragged blue T-shirt, faded khaki cargo shorts, and flip-flops. He holds a rake in his left hand and extends his right hand to shake mine, introducing himself.

"Diène N'dour," he says, smiling. "Come sit down in the shade." The toothy grin that lights up his dark face is contagious, and I find myself returning it in kind as I explain that I was looking for a place to spend the night.

"The accommodations are very simple," he says, surprising me, in English. I expected him to speak Serer, like the others in the village. How does he know my mother tongue? "The village has no electricity, and we get all our water from wells."

I look around the property from where we sit in palm-wood chairs under the mango tree. There are four huts, two on either side of the property, and near the front gate is a larger building with a thatched roof. I notice a well next to the larger hut, a few plastic buckets overturned next to it. Growing on the side of one hut is a massive bougainvillea plant, its bright magenta flowers cascading down the side of the hut. Along the edges of the property is a well-maintained garden with cacti and large green plants that flower bright yellow and purple. The *campement* seems empty, and as I look around I think to myself it would be a great place to write. Since traveling, I've found myself compelled to record all the details of my trip. The sights and sounds are so new to me, I want to capture them before I forget.

"Do you have room for me?" I ask.

"Yes, you stay," he says. His gaze holds mine, and I am unable to turn away. My cheeks feel flushed.

"You will stay a long time." He pauses. "*Inshallah.*"

I open my mouth to explain I only plan to stay one night, that I am on my way to Gambia, and that I am really just passing through. But a single word intercepts all the others.

"*Inshallah,*" I repeat. God willing.

* * *

I have a layer of grime to wash off after a day of traveling and ask Diène where I can take a shower. He walks over to the well, tosses in a bucket held on thick rope, and pulls up a bucket full of water, pours it into a larger bucket, and repeats this three times. He carries the full bucket towards the hut he offered to me for my stay, explaining this is my shower water.

"There is a bathroom in your hut," he says. "When you are finished, we can go to my mother's house. She will be happy to welcome you to our house for Christmas dinner."

"Thank you, but I'll just get some eggs and bread at the boutique." I have been eating egg sandwiches for days and would rather skip dinner than eat another one. But I think of Christmas dinner back home, and what an odd thing it would be to bring a complete stranger to the family holiday. "I have some writing to do."

"Katie," he pleads. "It is Christmas! My mother has cooked her best and would be honored to have you eat with us. Please come. It is our *teranga.*"

For the second time that day, I open my mouth to protest but words fail me.

"Thank you," I say. "It will be wonderful to meet your family."

After my shower, and when the afternoon heat has passed, we walk to his mother's house. The small, fenced-in plot of land holds three cement huts with palm leaf roofs, a few mango trees, and an assortment of farm animals.

Under the largest mango tree in the yard, a group of more than ten people are sitting and talking. When we walk over, each of them smiles warmly and immediately comes to shake my hand as Diène introduces me. Between the numerous exchanges of greetings, I fail to notice that a young girl has brought out a large bowl of *yassa poulet*, chicken with onion sauce and rice.

As a vegetarian, I try not to let my compassion for the natural world supercede my compassion for fellow human beings. Rather than announce that I refuse to eat the meal that is offered to me in a gesture of hospitality, I poke around with my spoon, looking for spoonfuls of rice that seem to be chicken-free. When I feel chunks of flesh in my mouth, I discreetly spit them out and fold them into the hem of my T-shirt.

After eating, we spread out comfortably on the plastic mats in the shade and spend the rest of the evening talking and drinking *attayah*. When Diène and I leave to go back to the *campement*, the moon is high and the night has come in. I pretend to say good-bye to the family dogs (crazy American, talking to farm animals!) and empty the chicken stash from my T-shirt into their eager mouths.

"Diène," I say before veering towards my hut, "thank you so much for sharing your family with me today."

"It is *teranga*," he says. "Maybe some day you will have the chance to do the same for me."

"*Inshallah*," I respond.

* * *

The next day, we sit in the kitchen, two strangers, looking through his family photos. Beams of the afternoon sun are streaming through holes in the thatched roof. One ray of sunlight, which was shining on us this morning, has shifted to the other side of the blue mosaic-tiled table. It illuminates the end of the baguette we shared for breakfast hours ago, now left to go stale next to our empty coffee cups.

"This is Ghandi," he says, flipping to the next photo in his pile.

I expect to see another friend or family member, but when I look at the photo I see a black and white goat staring back at me.

"Ghandi?" I ask. "You named your goat Ghandi?"

"Yes." He points up at a painting hanging on the kitchen wall of Ghandi, the peacemaker. "Just like the Mahatma. You know Mahatma Ghandi?"

"Yes," I answer, still confused.

"Well," he says. "Don't you think they have the same eyes?"

I look over at him and notice, for the first of what will be countless times, the way his cheeks dance with expression when he smiles. Laughter bubbles up from the spring of my heart and I feel time stop. I laugh until tears well in my eyes and my abdomen aches so much that I grip my stool to avoid falling.

It is, of course, too late. I have already fallen, hard.

CHAPTER 10

A Grapefruit Calendar

E verything that is planted in Yayeme grows," Diène tells me as we walk on the outskirts of the village. "We are lucky farmers here." He is showing me his family's fields, which are indistinguishable from the other sandy fields at the moment. He tells me that in a matter of months, they will be lush with millet plants. "Maybe you will still be here to see it," he says.

I laugh, but at this point, it doesn't seem too far-fetched. While I intended to leave Yayeme after only a day, it has been over a week. My Gambian visa will remain unstamped in my passport, and I have no plans to leave Yayeme until my vacation is over.

We walk down a well-worn path through the dusty fields; I learned a moment ago that if I stray off of it, burrs and other invisible prickers await. Diène doesn't seem to feel them, the soles of his feet calloused from a childhood of running around outside barefoot. Ahead of me, I see only four colors: the sandy color of the soil, which covers everything with a layer of dust, the green of palm fronds towering above us, the dirty white of the grazing cattle distant in the field, and the blue of the sky which extends all the way to the horizon.

"People all over the region know us as the Village of the Coconut Trees," Diène explains. As we walk back towards the village, these wild trees, *les cocotiers*, are sprouting up throughout the fields. Was it yesterday that we ate coconut meat and drank its juice, or the day before?

My days are blending together. Along with my compulsion to

plan, the accompanying sense of having wasted time, or used it un-productively, has completely disappeared. Time, like the Yayeme sunshine, has become a constant that I have stopped thinking about. Any time I ask someone what time it is, they answer one of three things: morning, afternoon, or night.

In the past few days, I've gotten to know this man walking beside me and I feel like I've met a kindred spirit. While he's never left Senegal, Diène has worked for five years welcoming international travelers and has a rich worldview and an appreciation of multi-culturalism. He speaks five languages fluently, and remnants of several more, all picked up simply from talking to the people that he meets. He is the first man in Senegal whose company I can tol-erate for more than a few hours, simply because he has pursued nothing more than a friendship. I am totally enraptured by his dis-interest in marrying me.

As we return to the village, the landscape gains color the mo-ment we see other people. Against the dull cement brick wall of a boutique on the edge of the village squats an old woman, a bright blue plastic bucket held between her knees. She is dressed in a loose yellow and pink top with an embroidered, square, ample neckline that falls off her shoulder. Her feet peek out of a match-ing yellow skirt, revealing blue plastic flip-flop sandals. Wrapped on her head is a piece of green tie-dyed fabric. When she sees us, she smiles, waves, and her face becomes the brightest thing around.

"Diène N'dour," she calls. We walk over to say hello, and she and Diène talk for awhile in Serer.

A young woman walks from around the corner of the boutique, dressed in stone-washed jeans and a tight-fitting neon orange tank top. Silver hoop earrings sparkle, reflecting light in various direc-tions. She carries a cooler and is selling cold *bissap* juice. I buy three juices and she hands us plastic yellow bottles with the slushy juice inside. In between gulps of the sweet refreshment, I examine the recycled bottle. The lettering on the outside is flaking off, but I can still make out enough words to understand that this bottle once held auto brake fluid. On the back of the bottle, in small print, I see a faded warning. *"Danger! Do not ingest contents of this bottle."*

We finish our juice and hand back the bottles. Diène and I say good-bye and continue our walk.

"Diène N'dour," the old woman calls after us. "Come eat dinner with my family. We are making *maffe*. Bring your *toubab* friend and I will fatten her up." She smiles and laughs, and Diène shouts over his shoulder that we will come.

The barrage of dinner invitations from complete strangers that I receive in Yayeme feel much safer than those in the big capital city, Dakar. In a village of less than 2,000 the idea that the person asking me is a friend of a friend is reasonable. In Dakar, a city of over one million inhabitants, accepting such an offer feels risky.

As we make our way into the village, more color gradually dots the landscape. The tie-dyed head wraps of a group of women waiting by the well. The bright plastic buckets at their feet. Colored T-shirts on the children encased in a cloud of orange dust kicked up by their own feet. A green, beaded necklace on a girl walking home with a block of soap in one hand and change jingling in the other. A bright, white, lacy blanket used to tie an infant to his mother's back. The magenta of bougainvillea flowers growing next to the boutique. The yellow of bananas in a basket propped on a table outside for sale.

In Yayeme, the landscape is simple, the decorations of homes and buildings modest. The eyes are drawn to two things: other people and the natural world we live in. This dual focus is reflected, also, in the lifestyles of these farmers who focus their energy on the cultivation of love in the heart of a neighbor and the millet or peanuts in the soil of the fields.

"Katie," says Diène, "I am glad you stayed in Yayeme. The sun is shining brighter since you arrived."

I look over at him, fiddling with a cigarette and lighter in his hands. I don't know what to say, so I smile at him until he looks at me. Reflexively, I look away, and feel my cheeks flush.

We mosey through the village, stopping to chat with everyone that we pass. All of them offer me something: an invitation to eat together, a bracelet from their wrist, a clip from their hair, a promise to come over and show me their photo album. Those who have nothing material to offer are generous with their most valuable asset of all: their time. Since arriving in Yayeme, my days have become full because I have started to measure them by interactions with people instead of minutes. I finally understand what Zator meant when he said time is an illusion.

By late afternoon, we arrive at our destination: a friend's fruit orchard that Diène wants to show me. We walk through the gate and as far as my eye can see are rows of fruit trees: oranges, lemons, grapefruits, coconut, cashews, deetax (a round green fruit), bananas, guavas, palm dates, papaya, and mangoes. We walk meditatively through the rows, Diène reluctant when I insist on climbing the grapefruit tree.

"You don't understand how much I love grapefruits," I yell down from the top. "I could eat all of them on this tree and still want more." I toss one more down, adding to the lot that Diène is carrying in the makeshift pouch of his T-shirt.

I count the tennis-ball-sized, yellow fruits. I know they are half the size of the ones back home, but twice as juicy and tart.

"Six!" I say. "Two a day and that should last me the rest of my days in Yayeme." In an instant, the joy of the grapefruits is gone and replaced by the sad realization that my vacation will be over in a few days. Tomorrow is New Year's Eve and university classes may (or may not) be starting next week. My Wolof classes start back up at the Baobab Center on Monday, only a few days from now.

"The tree gives fruit all season," Diène says quietly. Then he shouts to the treetop. "Take more—as many as you can."

I comply and lob down more, hoping each one will buy me some time.

CHAPTER 11

Women's Work

By rural Senegalese standards, I am a man. Sure, I wear traditional *pagnes*, long cotton wrap skirts, and occasionally a *fular*, a matching piece of fabric wrapped around my hair, but I don't do any work around the house. I spend my time choosing activities of leisure such as writing in the hammock, drinking tea at friends' houses, or walking to the boutique for snacks and drinks.

When I hear the rooster crow in the morning, followed by the calls from fisherwomen selling last night's catch, I roll over to go back to sleep. I do not worry about buying fish for tonight's dinner, because I know someone else will cook it for me. I do not plan how much water I need for the day's showering, drinking, and washing because someone else has gone to the well and drawn up a bucket for me. All day long, I am served food and drinks before others around me, and then someone else cleans up after me. This life of leisure is very manly.

All of my friends are men, because they seem to be the gender with enough free time to sit around with friends, drinking tea, smoking, and talking about current affairs. The women are too busy working. Pulling clean water from the well and delivering it to their families. Collecting firewood and managing the cooking fire in the kitchen. Pounding millet and grain in a mortar with a tall, wooden pestle. Budgeting for the weekly allotment of rice. Skinning and frying fish. Serving three hot meals a day. Washing dishes. Hand-washing their family's laundry. Feeding the livestock.

Breast-feeding babies. Educating toddlers and managing the chores of the eldest children. Devoting quality time to husbands.

Quite frankly, I think being a Senegalese woman would wipe me out, but I have a small problem. I miss the company of women. I long for the way I can say anything I am feeling to another woman, and have her listen like she understands. Not to mention that I spent my entire undergraduate career as a Women's Studies major fighting the patriarchy, and here in Senegal, I have become the patriarchy.

I realize that if I want to make any girlfriends, I have to get to work, literally. The women who I know never sit still or have idle time to chat.

On New Year's Eve, I have my first chance. I am sitting with a group of three men outside in the dark, a kerosene lamp on the table between our chairs, wishing one another a year of health and prosperity. Diène announces that he has decided to slaughter one of his two chickens to celebrate the New Year with a good meal and good friends.

"I will call for Mariama," says Musa, referring to his teenage daughter. "She is an excellent cook." Since I met Musa my first day in Yayeme and he walked me to the *campement*, I've seen him almost every day. He was not lying when he said Diène was a friend of his, and he comes over often to drink tea or chat. He is a father of ten, who makes his living as a farmer growing millet and peanuts. By no means is he a rich man, but by Yayeme standards he is doing okay. He has enough money to provide food and shelter for dozens of extended family members, he owns a horse and cart, and he has enough extra cash to indulge a penchant for gambling.

Tonight, before the sun set and the kerosene lamp became our only light source, he was reviewing the latest horse race results with his brother, Coly. The newspaper that printed the results was a few days old, but the results were still hot news; Musa's son had brought them from Fimela today. While the two men discussed the results, Musa copied several columns of numbers into a small notebook he had in his shorts pocket. This is the only time I've seen anyone other than me write anything down in Yayeme.

After almost an entire page was filled with numbers, Musa had chosen his horse and excused himself to go home and send his son to Fimela, the slightly larger village one mile down the road, with the modern conveniences of electricity, a newspaper stand, and a bookie.

Now Musa is walking back after placing his proxy bet, and he is with his daughter Mariama, the cook he has offered. Mariama carries a knife and bucket in one hand. Her infant son, Babu, is held on her back by a piece of fabric wrapped tightly around him with the two ends tied together across her breasts, flattening them to her chest.

"Diène N'dour," she says after greeting everyone. "Let me cook your chicken."

I stand up out of my chair abruptly, and all three men look at me.

"I am going to help Mariama," I say. "As a way to thank Diène." The men all voice their agreement. Diène gets up and leads Mariama through the kitchen building and back outside while I feel around for my flashlight on the table, hidden in the shadows cast by the lantern's flame.

When I catch up to the two of them, I shine my light on Diène, bending over a brown and white mass of feathers. The rooster struggles to get free until Diène steps on its feet and presses his long fingers across its chest. The rooster's yellow eyes bulge out of its red head, and Diène motions for Mariama to pass him the knife. The last thing I see before I turn my head is Diène's arm, raised level with his shoulder, start to descend.

My stomach clenches and I start to gag. I know if I don't swallow hard I will throw up everywhere, not only making for an awkward moment but, more important, ruining my chances to befriend Mariama through quotidian domestic chores.

"Katie," Mariama says. "Will you help me boil the water to feather the bird?" Diène kneels next to the limp bird, directing the blood pouring from its neck stub into a small hole dug into the sand.

"Actually, I'm going to the boutique to get onions and potatoes," I say after a moment. "Do we need anything else?"

"Good idea," she says. "Buy a Maggi spice cube." How could I forget Maggi, the bouillon that makes it into most meals? Mariama pauses. "Diène, do you have any oil?"

"*Xaa*," he says in Serer, shaking his head but not looking up from his butchering.

"Get a bag of oil, too," says Mariama. In order to make them affordable, shopkeepers partition household items and sell them in small plastic bags. This makes items such as cooking oil, tobacco, kerosene, pepper, salt, and laundry detergent affordable for the families who may only have a few CFA in hand. To buy a bottle of cooking oil when you only need a few ounces today (and lack storage safe from hungry farm animals or the heat's spoilage) is imprudent; the American philosophy of buying in bulk is absolutely absurd here.

I walk past the closest boutique and continue to the one a few hundred meters away with a generator and a working cooler. I buy bags of about one ounce of salt and pepper each, an eight-ounce bag of oil, three kilograms of potatoes, one kilogram of onions, a Maggi spice cube, and a cold bottle of Coke. I ask the man behind the counter to open the bottle and then sit outside drinking it, slowly. I don't want to return until that bird looks like the fleshy mounds covered in saran wrap that I hurry past in the deli section of the grocery store back home.

* * *

"Careful," Mariama says. "You are cutting away half the potato. The goats will be well-fed tonight."

I delegated myself the task of peeling potatoes when I got back from the boutique. The only available knife in the kitchen was a dull butter knife, so I grabbed the Swiss army knife out of my backpack. Now I am trying to remove only the peel from the dimpled potatoes, but sometimes the thick pulp of the potato stays attached to the peel, and I don't scrape it off into a salvage pile like Mariama has been doing. Instead, I toss the fleshy peel into the compost pile, from which the goats will dine tonight. Rationing potatoes is not a habit of mine, but I slow down to try and improve my peeling.

"Mariama," I ask, "do you like being a mother?"

"Of course!" she laughs, as if the answer were painfully obvious.

"It must be hard work though," I say. "Taking care of Babu and helping your own mom."

"It would be easier if I were married," she says. She turns back to the pan of chicken frying in hot oil on the gas burner and gives it a little stir with a wooden spoon. "My father won't allow it. He doesn't like Babu's father."

"Why not?" I ask. I hope I am not pushing my limits, but this is the kind of girl talk I have been craving.

Mariama is forthcoming. When she was sixteen she began working at a hotel in Ndangane, the nearby touristy village on the coast. She cooked, cleaned rooms, and flirted with an older coworker. They fell in love and within a few months, Mariama realized she was pregnant.

She comes from a fecund matrilineage: her own mother has ten children, and her twenty-year-old sister already has a baby. Ashamed of her behavior (sex outside of marriage is a no-no for her Muslim family) and terrified of her father's reaction, she told only her boyfriend. He did the right thing and promised to marry and support her. When Mariama could no longer hide her pregnancy, Musa, her father, was furious. He forced her to quit her job in Ndangane, forbid her to see or communicate with her boyfriend, and refused his blessing for the marriage.

"Now I stay at home and help my mother," Mariama says. "Sometimes Babu's father will come to see me, but my father won't allow him in our house. We are in love, but my father doesn't care."

"Why don't you move out?" I ask. It seems like a viable option I would propose to a friend at home if she were caught in a similar situation.

Mariama looks up from the pan of hot oil and stares blankly at me.

"To where?" she asks.

"Go marry your boyfriend and live in Ndangane," I say. "Your father will eventually come around."

"I can't do that," she says. "Where would I go without my family?" Babu wakes up and starts fussing. Mariama turns her head around to look down her back at Babu and murmurs softly to him. She leans over slightly and gently bounces Babu on her back. The glow of the kerosene lantern backlights her profile. Her chubby cheeks match those of her son, and she looks almost young enough to have baby fat left to lose. She glances over at me.

"Is your father hard to live with, too?" she asks.

"I don't live with my father anymore," I say. "I lived in a house with some friends—guys and girls—before I came to Senegal."

Mariama stands up straight again. Babu has settled back to sleep. She takes a pile of chopped onions and throws them into the pot and then eyes my pile of potatoes; I am working slowly. She grabs the unpeeled potatoes and, using the dull butter knife, starts peeling three potatoes for every one that I do. After a few moments of silence, she speaks.

"You are very lucky in America," she says. "You are free to disobey your fathers."

* * *

The next day, I am over at Mariama's house, sitting inside the master bedroom hut where her parents, Musa and Astou, sleep on a small foam mattress pad on a creaky wire bedframe. Right now, the bed is doubling as a couch for Diène and me. We accepted Musa's invitation to come over and drink *attayah*, Senegalese tea. A few minutes after we arrive, Musa's brother, Coly, walks into the hut, shakes our hands, and then gives Musa a blister pack of pills. Musa turns them over in his hands, and the two of them talk for a few minutes in Serer.

I zone out, looking through the open doorway, where I can see Astou sitting in the shade of the porch of another hut, starting to wash laundry. As she dunks dirty clothes into a basin of soapy water, and I sit with all the men in her house drinking tea, I wonder if any of the men in the room with me have ever washed their own laundry.

"Katie, do you know what these are?" Musa asks me, holding out the sheet of small white pills. I've earned myself a reputation as a drug user and dispenser in Yayeme. One day I offered a neighbor complaining of a headache some ibuprofen, and I poured the two pills out of my giant 500 count bottle, bought from Sam's Club before I left home. Word got out that I had pain-relieving drugs, enough for the whole village. Ever since, with some regularity, Senegalese friends come to find me with complaints of headaches, toothaches, fevers, and other ailments easily cured by ibuprofen.

The nearest clinic is a day's bus ride from Yayeme, in Josman, and is run by Catholic nuns and funded by missionaries. Even though the charge for care is minimal, the associated bus fare, prescription costs, and lab fees are too expensive for most Yayemeoise. Modern medicine as simple as ibuprofen is a luxury far out of reach.

I peer at the sheet of pills. On the back there is a label stamped on, written in French but easy enough to translate.

"This is amoxicillin," I say. "It's a pretty basic antibiotic."

"Do you know what it does?" he asks. Musa, Coly, and Diène are all looking at me with eyes full of faith.

"Well, if you get sick because of an infection, this will kill the infection."

Musa seems satisfied, but still deeply concerned.

"Astou!" he shouts. *"Gere meke."* I watch as Astou drops the shirt she is washing in the tub of water, puts her hands on her thighs, and pushes herself up into a standing position. She lumbers over, moving slower than usual.

I don't know who these pills are for, but of the bunch, my money is on Musa. Since I've known him, the only time I have seen him not smoking is during coughing fits. He smokes Marlboro cigarettes, hand rolled black tobacco cigarettes, *cali* joints, and any combination of the three. Once when I complained about not being able to sleep because of the heat, Musa was extremely empathetic. "Me too! I got up four times in the night to smoke."

When Astou arrives in the hut, Musa explains something to her briefly. Then he looks at me.

"Katie, can you explain again what these do?" he asks.

"It kills infections that make you sick," I say to Astou, who is staring at a patch of floor right beside me. Her French is as limited as my Serer, so our conversations have never matured beyond greetings. "A few months ago, I had a chest infection with a bad cough. I took pills like these to get better."

Musa raises an eyebrow with new interest, but I can tell he's not gotten the answer he was looking for. He looks at Astou, who does not look back at him. She seems perfectly healthy to me. Tired, maybe, but less so than I would be after all the work that she does.

"What does it do for women?" he asks.

"It works the same on men and women," I say. "Is everything all right?"

"Oh, yes, yes," he says. "Astou just has a…uh, a…an infection." He looks at me to see if he chose the right word. "She went to the clinic and they gave her this. We're not sure if it will work."

"Well, it might," I say. "I hope you feel better, Astou."

She smiles at the sound of her name, and then goes back to her laundry. I suddenly feel awkward sitting in the hut, so I excuse myself to look for Mariama. Musa walks me over to her hut, letting me know that she might be sleeping.

"It's nice of you, Katie, to spend time with Mariama," Musa says in French as we stop at the hut's doorway. "I hope you understand her; she left school too early, was never a good student. She doesn't even speak French." I am puzzled; Mariama's French is flawless and has never given me any trouble.

I walk in the hut and find Mariama lying down in her bedroom, breastfeeding Babu. Her older sister is sitting on the end of the bed, holding her own sleeping baby. Mariama has given Babu her pinky to grasp with his tiny little fist, which he clenches in pulses.

"Katie," Mariama says in a deep voice, mocking the accent of her father. "I hope you can understand me, with my bad French." Mariama and her sister both burst into a fit of laughter, muffled for the babies' benefit.

"He was just confusing your French with mine," I say. "I'm the one who needs help."

"Our father is always confused," says Mariama's older sister. "He has too many children to know them all."

"Maybe I could move out of his house, like you suggested, Katie," Mariama says. "He may never notice." I gaze at Babu, his pudgy little mouth suckling nourishment from his mother until he is fast asleep. Mariama gently sits up, leaving him asleep on the bed.

"He is so beautiful, Mariama," I whisper. "His father must be a very handsome man."

"Oh, Katie. You wouldn't believe how handsome! He is all I see when I look at Babu."

The three of us chat until Astou calls Mariama and her sister to come help hang the laundry. In unison, like school children putting on backpacks before leaving their classroom, Mariama and her sister put their sleeping babies on their backs and wrap blankets around them, securing them by tying the ends tightly across their chests.

As we walk out, I pop my head back into the bedroom hut to say good-bye to the men, who are sitting in a thick haze of cigarette smoke and drinking tea.

Heading back to the *campement*, I get about thirty yards away when I hear Musa shouting my name. He is motioning for me to come to the fence, where he is standing.

"Katie," he says in a lowered voice. " I have one more question to ask you about the pills."

"Sure. What is it?" I say.

"You say those are antibiotics," he says. "For infections."

"Yes."

"They are not the pills a woman takes when she is pregnant and doesn't want to be?"

I am rendered speechless. I certainly do not know how to say abortion in Wolof, and never imagined I would have to. I wonder if Astou asked the Catholic missionaries at the Josman clinic for those pills in French, Wolof, or Serer. Did it matter?

"No, Musa," I say. "I am sorry. They're just antibiotics."

"Okay," he says quickly, rushing through his words. "I just wanted to know, thank you." He awkwardly puts out his hand for me to shake, which I do.

"Come over for dinner tonight," he insists. "Astou is cooking *maffe*, she'd be happy to serve you."

CHAPTER 12

Telecommunications

Therey are moments when I am sitting in the shade of a fruit tree in the peace of rural Senegalese life and I try to imagine how the villagers reacted the first time they saw a white European arrive at their doorstep. If the present is any indication of the past, my guess is that they invited them to share tea and take a load off, offering them what they could to help them in their journey.

Late one morning, on one of my last days in Yayeme, after spending an hour lying in the hammock, watching two pigeons weave a nest in the branches above, I hear Musa shout a familiar phrase over the gate of *Daam Sa Doole*.

"*Njape, gere meke,*" he calls. I watch Diène walk over to the gate and open up both doors. A white Peugot van enters slowly into the *campement*, driven by two tourists. For a moment, I am taken aback. I haven't seen other white people in over a week.

"*Katie, je te present Franc et Isabella,*" Diène says, bringing the couple over from their parked van.

"*Bonjour. Enchanté,*" I say, my voice shaky. I am still self-conscious speaking French with the French. The Senegalese, who speak an average of four or five languages each, are more forgiving of my numerous grammatical errors.

Franc is tall and rail thin. A burning cigarette balances on his lower lip as he extends his hand to me. Although he is not inhaling, his pronounced cheekbones give the impression that he is. His mousy brown hair is in dreadlocks, pulled back by a bandana of red, green, and yellow. I recognize it as the kind sold in Dakar along with soccer jerseys and other sports paraphernalia. On the front of his sun-faded black T-shirt is an upside-down question mark, the yellow ink cracking with age.

Hiding behind him is Isabella, with black hair that hangs down past her shoulders. It is unkempt and frizzy enough to make me wonder when she last saw a mirror. In that mop of hair, I can see several thin braids, some with a colorful ribbon, others with beads. While Franc appears to be no older than 30, Isabella's olive face is leathery and sun damaged, easily putting her at age 45. She wears a loose black tank top over a long Bohemian skirt so threadbare that with the sun shining from behind her, I can see the outline of her legs. She looks like a woman who has spent most of her time at street carnivals, hawking whatever sells.

"*Enchanté,*" she says with a thick accent. Her broad smile reveals a mouth full of stained teeth, with a wide gap between the first two.

"Please sit down," says Diène, gesturing to the empty seats around me.

"Not yet," says Franc, turning to look at Diène. "We still need to discuss price."

"Yes, we will," says Diène. "But I thought I would first get you some water. You two must be thirsty after your long ride from Dakar."

Franc snorts, a sound somewhere between a laugh and a scoff.

"Right, and then when the bottles are dry, you will charge me 3,000 CFA for each," Franc says. "Do not take us for fools; we have been here in Africa for weeks."

Diène grins and clasps his hands together, bringing them up to rest under his chin.

"I do not know which parts of Africa you have visited, but here in Yayeme, bottled water only costs 500 CFA." He moves over to one of the chairs and places his hands on top of the back, gently tapping it. "Why don't you two just rest a while?"

Franc takes out a rolled cigarette from the pouch in his pocket and lights it with the burning cigarette in his mouth. He throws the butt from his mouth into the sand at his feet and inhales the new cigarette.

Isabella startles me by taking the seat to my left. She has managed to walk behind the commotion without making a sound and sit next to me. She smiles widely again, and tips her pack of cigarettes towards me with raised eyebrows. I shake my head and smile.

She shrugs her shoulders and tosses her head, throwing the blanket of hair off of her right shoulder, onto her left.

Diène and Franc step out of earshot and continue to discuss. By the time Isabella is halfway through her third cigarette, they come over and Franc sits down.

"I am going to the store for some water. Does anybody need anything?" Diène asks. Isabella flips the lid on her box of Marlboros.

"Cigarette?" She shakes her box and I see three remaining cigarettes bang into each other. Her accent, clearly not native French, puts me at ease. She'd probably turn her head the other way when I confused *le* and *la*.

As soon as Diène leaves, Franc begins the inquisition.

"Katie," he says. "Where are you here visiting from?"

"Dakar," I respond. I am in no hurry to share with this guy. His beady blue eyes stare directly into mine, trying to pierce their way into the truth of the matter.

"Are you traveling through West Africa, then?"

"No. I live in Dakar."

"But clearly, you are not Senegalese." With each question, he leans further towards me.

"English is my first language."

"*Voila!*" he says, straightening up. "*Tu es Americanne! Une soldat de l'armie de George Bush!*" American? Yes. A soldier in Bush's army? I see where this is going.

I don't respond; instead, I begin eyeing Isabella's pack of Marlboros on the table, wishing I had accepted her offer. She has one leg draped over the arm of her chair, and she is staring vacantly at the hut behind me.

"Katie," says Franc. "What do you think of George Bush?"

"He is our president." I am not going to engage this guy.

"So, you are a Bush supporter then?"

"I didn't say that."

"So, you oppose his dictatorship and the bloody deaths that he has caused with it?"

"I didn't say that either."

"Well, you didn't have to. You know, most of this country is Muslim. You better watch yourself, walking around as an anti-Islam American. You could get yourself in trouble."

"I have found the Senegalese to be nothing but welcoming."

"And that is just what you want, isn't it? So you can bring your neo-colonial, capitalist empire to another corner of the world where you slowly kill the enemy with Coca-Cola and Marlboros. Recruit them for your wars..."

As he blathers on, I remember reading about *Thiaroye*.

During World War II, when France and the United States were allies, and relatives of Franc and mine who met on foreign soil may have been more amicable, hundreds of thousands of Africans enrolled in the French army. Some accounts say as many as half the French troops who landed in southern France in August 1944 came from Africa. Shortly after, a brigade of West African soldiers returned to Senegal at *Camp de Thiaroye*. Exhausted but victorious, they sang *Le Marseillaise*, their adopted national anthem, and congratulated one another on making it home alive to their families. When they were refused the promised wages by the French army, they protested and demanded to be paid. The French army rolled in quickly in army trucks and tanks and opened fire on the crowd, killing all the soldiers. Crowds of the soldiers' families, who had gathered to welcome them home, watched the massacre happen. Despite the French attempt to bury the incident, the oral tradition of Senegal kept it alive through story telling and songs. In 1989, Ousmane Sembène, the Senegalese writer, created a film, *Camp de Thiaroye*, documenting the incident. Now the rest of the world can witness the story that the Senegalese have been passing down from parent to child in story-telling circles for generations.

Franc is still lecturing, waving his cigarette in the air. One leg is crossed over the other, and his foot is tucked behind his calf, a surprisingly feminine posture.

"...to fill all of those oil barrels with blood." He pauses to light another cigarette.

"It must be true then," he says after taking a break. "What they say about *les ahme-reeee-cans*." He strings out each syllable. "They are *les amies des requins*."

He laughs in a way that tells me that he has just insulted me. The problem is that my limited vocabulary is failing me. I know *les amies des* means "friends of" but I have no idea what *requins* meant. I smile and, as Ibu has with the lyrics of Bob Marley, try to write the word in my memory until I can find a friend who can translate.

* * *

Isabella has broken her silence. She licks the pastis from her lips, having just finished her fifth shot glass of the anise-flavored liquor. Diène, Franc, Isabella, and I have spent the day together, touring around neighboring villages, and have ended up at a hotel bar on the beach in N'dangane, about ten miles from Yayeme. After a day with these two, I am happy to be slightly drunk. The bar manager, Johan, is a French man living in Senegal, and he connected instantly with Franc.

Isabella lifts her arms towards the sky and slides down off her barstool. A nest of black matted hair sprouts from her armpits, and I can see that she has braided two beads into each side. In a sultry voice, she sings in a language I don't recognize. Her body slithers along with the music, a snake being charmed out of a basket. She moves over to Franc, puts her hands on his thighs, and moves to whisper something in his ear. He listens for a minute, smiling, and then grabs the hair behind her head and yanks it hard, pulling her away from him.

"*Vas-y*," he commands. Go away. She moves her dance about ten feet from the bar.

"Where did you find such a wild Safari animal?" Johan asks Franc. He takes the white towel draped over his shoulder and wipes the inside of the glass that Isabella has just emptied. He fills it back up with pastis and puts it on the bar in front of her empty stool.

"Somewhere between Fès and Marrakech." He takes Isabella's glass from the bar and sips it. "A broke gypsy who needed a ride; she's found some creative ways to pay her way."

Franc has been narrating stories of his road trip all day. From Spain to Senegal, the geographic details of each story change, while the plot lines remain predictable. Franc arrives in an underdeveloped city where the only thing more abject than the poverty is the ignorance and laziness of its inhabitants. In his quest to survive among such savagery, Franc always manages to find the one decent bushman who can help him get what he needs (gas, food, lodging, women) although they always cheat him on the price.

"Johan," says Franc. "I do not understand. We paved the roads for them. We built their schools. We installed telephone lines. Why is it that now the only decent place I can find to call home is a French-owned hotel?

"Diène." Franc turns his head to look down the bar. "How on earth do you people stay in touch with one another?"

At the end of each of his stories, Franc turns to Diène and asks him an impossible question. Diène never answers but just stares ahead at the shelves lined with bottles of French liquor. This is just as good a response as any, because Franc never gives him time to answer before launching into his next story.

"Johan," Franc says. "Ask Diène how people here communicate

with one another."

"Diène is a good man," says Johan. "He brings all of his clients here to get drunk at my bar. He keeps my family back in France well-fed."

"*Chaqun à son goût*," says Franc. To each his own. He turns to Diène and continues. "You accepted our financial investments, our military protection, our education. But you still refuse our culture."

* * *

The next morning, a gut-wrenching wailing wakes me up. I sit up in bed, my head aching with hangover, and I tell myself it's a fish seller, trying a new marketing technique, but the pit deep in my stomach tells me otherwise. After a few minutes of hoping it will stop, I stumble out of my hut to find out what is going on. I find Franc, Isabella, and Diène have all done the same.

Over the shared wall of a fence in the back of the *campement* plot, I see the source of the audible sorrow. A girl in her late teens who has her eyes closed and head thrown back is producing the howl. Her face is scrunched up in pain and she has the hem of her shirt crunched in her hand. Periodically, when she stops for breath, she uses it to wipe her eyes dry.

"What happened?" asks Isabella. The four of us stand mesmerized by the scene.

"There has been a death," answers Diène. "That girl lost her mother last night."

"What happened?" repeats Isabella.

"She was sick; she was losing weight and it became hard for her to breathe. That is the oldest daughter; now she is the woman of the house."

The girl's wail has the piercing quality of lightning and the reverberations of thunder, rattling the chest of anyone who hears it. The village seems a vacuum of any noise other than the girl. Like drivers at an intersection yielding to a funeral procession, the chirping birds, braying donkeys, and chattering children let death trump their plans. I feel warm tears well up in my eyes.

"I wish she would shut the hell up," Franc says. "People die every day and some of us don't feel the need to broadcast it."

An older woman comes to comfort the girl, and the girl drapes her arms around the other's shoulders, her body going limp and collapsing on the ground. The wailing picks up strength.

"Franc," says Diène. "Last night you asked how we stayed connected to each other without telephones and the Internet.

"*Voila*," he gestures towards the girl. "Our telecommunications."

* * *

We wave good-bye to Franc and Isabella late that morning and Diène tells them to come back soon.

"Do you get a lot of tourists like that?" I ask.

"Like what?" he responds

I am at a loss for words. "Special."

"Katie," he says, "if God sends you people who need help, you can only serve them and believe that you will be rewarded by something bigger than both you and them."

"And if they are blind to the help you are giving them?" I ask.

"All the more for God to see," he says. With a smile he starts raking the fallen mango leaves into a pile, leaving a trail in the sand where the rake's teeth plow through. Tomorrow, people will have kicked sand over the fresh rake tracks and a new cover of leaves will have fallen. And Diène will wake up early to rake it all up again.

The next morning, I wake up early so that Musa's son can give me a ride on their horse and cart to Fimela, where I will take a taxi to Josman, where I will catch a bus to Dakar. It's an entire day of exhausting travel that I am not looking forward to. Diène and I have been debating all morning about whether he will accompany me to Dakar. He insists that it is the hospitable thing to do, and I tell him it's unnecessary. We compromise and agree he'll come all the way to Josman with me.

We are pretty quiet during the taxi ride, until I remember a question that's been written in my head for two days.

"Diène," I ask. "What does *requin* mean?"

"Uh," he thinks for a moment. "I am not sure, exactly. It is a naughty fish."

That makes me laugh.

"A naughty fish?" I repeat.

"Yes. Big teeth. Fast swimming. Makes trouble."

"A shark?" I ask.

"That's it," he says. "A shark."

For the rest of the car ride, I repeat the catchy pun in my head. *Les americains: les amies des requins.* It takes my mind away from how fast we are covering the distance to Josman.

In Josman, Diène and I sit on my oversized backpack on the side of the road waiting for the bus. He promises that he'll call me every day until I can find the time to come back and visit. I know this is not exactly the truth, but I also know the Senegalese believe that lies that build are better than truths that destroy. I promise I will do the same.

When I see the bus coming towards us, my heart sinks and tears well up in my eyes. Diène starts talking rapidly about how he really should come all the way to Dakar, it's not a big deal, it's what he wants to do. I interrupt him by wrapping my arms around him in a hug and pulling him towards me.

"This is only the beginning," I say.

I board the bus, giving my backpack to the porter who lugs it on to the roof of the bus. As the bus pulls away, I watch Diène waving. When his silhouette grows too small to see, I turn around and look at the road ahead.

LESSON 5

Ñak jeriñu
Sweat on the brow, a job enjoyed
Wolof Proverb

Jal ki jegg
Work it, have it
Serer Proverb

*Hard work pays off, and the Senegalese know
this. The rural families must work tirelessly during the
rainy season to feed their families for the rest of the year.
The city dwellers struggle to find paying work and are
grateful to have it. During the five years that it took to
bring Project Japalé Gouné from its inception to a
self-sustaining school lunch program, our work was
not always easy, but it was always enjoyable.*

CHAPTER 13

A Walk on the Beach

Project Japalé Gouné is born the day Natalie, Ling Ling, and I follow directions in our *Lonely Planet* guidebook to *Pointe des Almadies*, the western-most point of continental Africa. We decided that was geographically significant enough to warrant a special day trip. (It did not hurt that it was within walking distance of *Plage de N'Gor*, one of the best sunbathing beaches in the area.)

As a tourist destination, *Pointe des Almadies* is pretty boring, not much more than a big pile of black rocks. There is a pungent odor coming from the fishermen's drying racks: a trellis of fishing line woven between wooden posts. There are dozens of tiny fish hanging on each line, their stench enough to clear the beach of anyone but us. Half a mile south of us, down the coast, is a group of touristy restaurants, selling crepes and grilled fish.

The three of us scramble over the trail of rocks until we are thirty feet offshore. We perch atop the peak of a pyramid of large rocks, getting as far west as we can, and look down at the camera for the obligatory photo.

Ling Ling and I turn to walk back to shore, discussing lunch possibilities, while Natalie takes in the moment. She faces west, her arms outstretched, and yells to the white-capped ocean waves.

"This is the closest I will be to home in a year!"

Natalie, Ling Ling, and I are all Rotary Scholars, brought together by Natalie's gift of connecting people. Natalie had contacted both of us before we left the United States. On our shared flight to Dakar, Natalie was already telling me the details of Ling Ling's life in Dakar. Ling Ling had arrived in Dakar a few weeks before us with a Rotary Cultural Scholarship to study French for three months.

We walk down the beach and as the restaurants come into our focused view, they appear to be closed. We are only thirty feet from the group of empty stalls when a man says hello.

"*Bonjour, toubabs!*" he greets us, using the word for foreigners. "Come. Sit. Have a drink!" he says, a wide grin on his face.

Underneath a blue and white canvas tent is a single, round plastic table and four matching chairs. Marking the periphery of the crowded interior are potted tropical plants, narrow stems of broad leaves rising three feet high. In the far corner is the kitchen—a two-burner gas camping stove and a small cooler. We accept his invitation, and soon the smell of frying crepe batter and sugar is making us salivate.

"*Toubabs*," our waiter says as he serves our crepes and glass bottles of Fanta, "where are you from?"

"The United States," says Natalie.

"And you?" he points to Ling Ling.

"The United States," she says.

He looks at me.

"No—you are all from the same country?" He seems shocked. This has happened to us before here in a country so close-knit that physical characteristics as minute as eye shape can identify what family you come from. *Those deep-set eyes, you must be a Serer.* Is it N'dour or Coly? It is an anomaly that three people as different looking as us can call the same country home.

"You, yes." He points to me. "You are an American."

Then he shifts his gaze suspiciously at Natalie. Natalie stands tall at 5'10" but seems even taller, elongated by confidence. The product of a French Canadian mother and Haitian father, she is a beautiful, biracial woman with a magnetic presence that is trailed by the gazes of Senegalese men wherever she goes.

"You are *metisse* (biracial)," the waiter says to Natalie. "Maybe your mother is American, but you are certainly the daughter of an African." Her explanation that neither her father nor mother was American, or African, only adds to his disbelief.

He shifts his confident glance towards Ling Ling, a Chinese woman standing five feet tall.

"You are Japanese. Tell the truth. Look at you!" He crosses his arms smugly, and then leans forward with renewed interest. "Do you know Bruce Lee?"

These types of conversations no longer make us uncomfortable, but allow us to joke about representing the United Colors of Rotary. We constantly remind ourselves that racial identity politics are much less nuanced here. Black is African. White is American or European. And Asian is, well, Japanese. We laugh it off in order not to take offense.

We pay our bill and decide to walk to *Plage de N'Gor*, the beach. We cut through the outskirts of N'Gor village where out of the sand sprout gigantic beach homes and luxury hotels. It feels like a ghost town because most of the owners are back in Europe for the season and the houses are under construction. We haven't seen any other people, but I can smell wet handmade cement bricks drying in the sun.

We are talking about how lucky we are.

"Here we are, walking on the western shores of Africa," says Natalie. "Our only responsibility is to study and serve as Ambassadors of Goodwill. Thanks to Rotary, we don't have any financial worries. How great is life?"

"I feel indulgent some days," I respond. "Passing the *talibé* (child beggars) on the way to school every day, to get an education that I didn't even have to pay for."

"Ladies," starts Ling Ling. "Let's do something about it. We should start a project together, combine our passion for service, and give back to our new community. What do you say?"

"What do you have in mind?" I ask. Before anyone can respond, a traveling merchant selling children's clothes out of the basket balancing on his head interrupts us. His basket is piled high with folded neon clothes, and draped down the sides of the basket are pairs of socks strung together. In each hand he holds elegant, lacy children's dresses wrapped in plastic. The sheer magic of balancing all of his merchandise while walking stops us in our tracks and commands all of our attention.

"Clothes for sale! I am selling children's clothes!" he yells out to us. He stops and I can only stare at the heavy basket resting above his dry brow. Not even one drop of sweat.

"Hey, *toubabs*, you want to buy some clothes for your children?" he asks. "I have some really nice T-shirts, dresses, socks, and Nike shoes."

"No, thanks," says Natalie. "None of us have any children." He looks at us as suspects.

"I don't believe you. You are too old not to have children. Buy some clothes to bring to your babies back home." He stays put.

I recoil behind Natalie and Ling Ling, knowing I am weak against the persistent merchants of Senegal. When they ask me why I won't buy their merchandise, I ramble on and on, listing half-truths and sorry excuses that even I can see through. My chattering only weakens my resolve, and the wisest of the salesmen throw a punch directly to my weak spot: they tell me that the few dollars I am refusing to spend could feed their whole family dinner that night. What American can resist shopping as charity?

Natalie has a good defense against merchants. She seems to be strengthened by her own voice and is much less likely to buy her way out of an uncomfortable conversation. Seemingly without effort, she gets him to leave. He puts his basket back on his head and walks away. After a few yards, he pivots carefully around and shouts.

"*Toubabs*, you should all marry me." He outstretches his arms, the basket now balancing completely without his grip. "I will give you a dozen beautiful African babies." He flashes a bright white smile and laughs as he paces backwards, away from us.

"Do you think he means a dozen *each?*" asks Ling Ling, making us laugh. "Now, let's get back to our plan. What is a cause that we could support?"

I think of Brigitte and the way she broke that measly little morsel of a cookie in half in order to share.

"Well, since we all feel so grateful for our scholarships," I say, "maybe we could think of a way to give back to Senegalese students."

"I like that idea," says Natalie. "Give with gratitude."

"Me, too," says Ling Ling. "What is our first step?"

We walk a few steps, lost in thought, and then are snapped back to our surroundings by the squeals of children.

"*Toubab! Toubab! Toubab!*" Three young children, a boy and two girls all under the age of five, emerge from the half-finished foundation of a nearby mansion and run at us, full throttle. About ten feet from us, the two girls stop in their tracks and shoot us looks of intense curiosity, mirroring the look I gave the clothes seller.

The boy runs right up to us. He is equal parts adorable and disgusting. One hand is in his mouth, caked in a paste made of snot, sand, and saliva. On his shaved head, large bald spots indicate mange or malnutrition. From underneath his faded, tight T-shirt pokes his bloated potbelly. He is wearing no pants or diaper, but on his feet are two mismatched flip-flops—one too large and the other too small.

He is smiling ear to ear. His hand is thrust out to us, palm open, demanding a gift.

"*Bic. Bic. Bic.*" It always surprises me that Bic pens are the gift of choice for kids here, rather than money or candy. Some other tourists believe it is because education is so highly valued by and so out of reach for most children. I prefer to attribute it to a group of mothers, concerned about cavities and greed, who set out to make pens the coolest toy in town.

Behind the boy, the two girls are holding hands and taking deliberate steps toward us. The older is wearing a tattered T-shirt, at least three sizes too big, and she has a piece of scrap cloth wrapped around her waist as a skirt. The younger wears a dress that could have come off an American Girl doll that I donated to Goodwill when I was about ten years old. The pink lace on the collar and hem, once an opulent trimming, is now ripping off at the seams.

Behind the kids stands a tent made of plastic rice sacks tied together for walls, cowering in the shadow of the mansion. A woman is crouched down, molding wet sand and gravel into bricks by hand. The day's labor is drying behind her, laid out in twenty rows of fifty bricks each. She looks up at us, but her hands don't stop working.

Some tenets of capitalism stretch across the globe: the houses of the rich are built by poor migrant labor. This family was most likely from rural Senegal or a poor neighboring country such as Guinea or Mali, having come to Dakar looking for work. They had found it helping build a stranger's vacation home, while living in a tent made from their own garbage.

The little boy pulls his dirty hand out of his mouth, stretching a string of sandy saliva a few inches from his mouth until it breaks. He stretches his hand out to us, and I instinctively take a step back. Those germs.

Ling Ling, the easiest target among us because of her height, avoids the grubby handshake by squatting down next to the boy and shocking him with English.

"Aren't you cute? How old are you? Are these your sisters? Where do you live? Where are your pants?" Ling Ling turns to Natalie and me and, quite plainly says, "I want to clothe this child."

When Ling Ling says she wants to do something, she does it. Her excellence at making things happen is so palpable that we have started using her name as a verb. If you are stuck on the way to your goals, and you need to buckle down, create a solution, and work hard, you simply have to *lingling* the situation.

This incredible trait is even more remarkable considering Ling

Ling's start in the United States. As an infant, she traveled with her parents and brother from Vietnam to Hong Kong on a refugee boat so crowded that her mother had to hold her the entire trip. One morning, a crew member served breakfast by tossing out loaves of bread to the passengers. Delirious with exhaustion and hunger, Ling Ling's mother reached out her arms to catch the bread and dropped Ling Ling, who fell to the deck below. She landed into the squishy belly of a fat man, who could have been Uncle Sam himself, saving her from harm.

As their oversea voyage neared its end, Ling Ling's mother did what she could to have her family look their best upon arrival. Wanting them to wear clean shoes, she tied all of their shoes together with a piece of string and tossed the lot of them overboard into nature's washing machine. The string couldn't withstand the ocean current, and the whole bunch of their shoes floated away. Ling Ling and her family arrived in Hong Kong, where they would board a plane to the United States, barefoot.

And yet, Ling Ling would tell you this was a lucky start. She has committed her life's work to ending poverty through international economic development.

In her typical fashion, she launches into her plan. She shouts to the clothing salesman, only 50 yards ahead of us, to come back. "How much for the outfit you are holding?" she asks when he is within earshot.

"8,000 CFA," he responds. Sixteen bucks.

Everything in Senegal has three prices: the starting price, the real price, and the *toubab* price. The *toubab* price is best avoided or ignored.

"I will buy three outfits for 8,000 CFA," says Ling Ling.

"Ha!" The merchant laughs as he walks towards us. He takes the heavy basket off his head and lays it next to him. He picks out three outfits and hands them to Ling Ling. "Take these. Special price for you, 40,000 CFA."

"Oh, come on. Can you give me a deal? After all, I think you are right. I should have a lot of children."

The thing that always amazes me about bargaining, which can take an entire afternoon if it's an important enough purchase, is that the Senegalese never get upset. They may accuse you of being mean, cheap, and selfish; you may return with accusations of greed, thievery, and low-quality merchandise, but they will always wear a smile and appreciate a friendly joke. As Americans, we get impatient and uncomfortable and don't feel right until the deal is closed. For the Senegalese, it is never about the purchase. It is about the relationship.

After a few minutes of banter, Ling Ling gets a good price: three full outfits and a cute little dress for ten bucks. The merchant throws in an extra outfit as a gift, usually a sign that we should have invested more time in bargaining.

Ling Ling takes the little boy's hand and walks toward the woman making bricks, the rest of us following behind them. Ling Ling greets the mother and hands her the outfits, motioning that they are for the three kids.

The mother is visibly happy, but she doesn't skip a beat of work. After she expresses her thanks, it is clear that she does not speak Wolof. With few words in common to exchange and after a few moments of mutual admiration and smiling, we go on our way.

"Wow, Ling Ling. Way to go!" says Natalie. "Talk about putting your money where your mouth is."

"It's only $10," she says. "We spent more than that on lunch today."

"If you can clothe a family for $10, imagine what you could do with $100," I muse.

"How many students could we help with that?" asks Natalie.

"Well," says Ling Ling. "Let's find out."

CHAPTER 14

The Talibé

L et's take a cab back," Natalie suggests. "It's what? Like, one US dollar? Totally worth it today." We are leaving LGM, our favorite local restaurant that serves up familiar junk food like pizza, crepes, hamburgers, and ice cream. Best of all, they have central air-conditioning, which is difficult to leave today with the 90+ degree heat.

"Fine by me," says Ling Ling. "It might save my life." Ling Ling was the last of us to arrive at lunch, and when she came in she was visibly shaken up. Crossing a major intersection to get to the restaurant, she explained, she was within inches of being blind-sided by a speeding taxi. The one traffic rule in Dakar—where cars, buses, horse-pulled carts, motorcycles, bicycles, stray dogs, and pedestrians compete for space—seems to be that the biggest vehicle rules. At her height, Ling Ling hardly stands a chance.

Our lunch was with purpose: we wanted to develop our ideas on how to help Senegalese children. We talked for hours, adopting Senegalese time for our dining, and made definitive plans to move forward on our project. We decided that no matter how our efforts manifested, there were three goals that would serve as our guide. Like the hunter moving *ndank, ndank* through the forest, we wanted to have a clear target in focus.

The first goal was to give the gift of education to students in Dakar, as a way to pay forward the financial support from Rotary Foundation that made our studies in Senegal possible. Earlier in the week, Ling Ling had shared our initial ideas with her Wolof

instructor with the hope of getting some advice on how to connect with a local school. This opened what would be floodgates of
serendipity: one of her instructor's best friends was the principal
of the elementary school in our neighborhood, *L'Ecole Primaire de
Point E* (Point E Elementary School).

Second, we agreed that our ultimate goal would be sustainabil-
ity. In other words, we wanted our gift to provide an ongoing program or service that could eventually be maintained without
additional funds from us. If we only raised enough money for a
one-time gift, we wanted it to be a lasting gift—buying textbooks
for the school library may have a greater impact than paying one
semester of tuition for a student who would be unable to continue
the following semester for lack of continued funds. In the same vein,
if we raised enough money to build a program or service, we wanted
to be clear from the beginning that we intended for the school's in-
volvement to grow over time until they took it over completely.

Third, we wanted to demonstrate "Service Above Self"—the
motto of Rotary International. After all, they were responsible for
bringing us together and, by accepting our scholarships, we had
all agreed to represent Rotary as well as we could by putting service
to others above ourselves.

Our next steps were to visit the school and ask the staff what
the biggest needs were for their poorest students. All of this, of
course, could come only after we hailed a cab and negotiated a fair
price for the ride back home.

Now, Natalie leans in to the passenger-door window of the cab
that pulls up. There are spiderwebs of cracks all over the windshield
and a huge dent in the rear passenger door. From where I stand, I
can see that the inside of the cab is typical of all others—all of the
paneling, window levers, and handles on the doors have been
stripped away, leaving nothing but the metal door frame. Natalie
lets out an exasperated *"Dedet!"* or no, and the taxi drives away.

"He was asking 3,000 CFA," she says as she turns back to us.
In a moment, another taxi comes, and the negotiations go much

smoother. In a minute, the three of us are crowded together in the back seat and Natalie starts retelling the story of her host family's recent pig slaughter for a holiday feast. I've heard it a few times before and stare out the window to let my mind wander.

A block or two later, we approach a red light at a busy intersection, and the moment we stop, the *talibé* start their work. The *talibé* are child beggars, almost always boys, who come up to stopped-car windows and weaken passengers' reserve with their big, brown, puppy-dog eyes. They shake empty tomato-paste tins, imploring the people to fill them with spare change or extra food.

The only thing more disheartening than their well-practiced forlorn facial expressions is knowing that many of these boys are working for a master, an adult ring-leader who lures street children with promises of a better life, but then forces them to work all day as beggars, giving them only enough food to keep them alive for the next day. According to a study released in February 2008 by the International Labour Organization, the United Nations Children's Fund, and the World Bank, there are at least 7,600 child beggars working the streets of Senegal. The children collect an average of 300 CFA a day, just 72 cents.

At one time, the *talibé* were not a sign of exploitation, but rather one of learned humility. They were students enrolled in an Islamic school, sent to beg for their first meal of the day to learn humility, in line with Islamic tradition and education. Sadly, most of these children today will never see the inside of any school.

I grimace as I see two boys approach my window; saying no makes me feel cold-hearted, but I don't want to support the begging ring. If I have food, I will share it but I don't want to give money. As the taller of the two boys rests his hand on the car's roof and peers at me, my hands fidget with the purse in my lap, my gaze fixed at the back of the driver's headrest. The shorter boy tucks himself under the armpit of the older boy; his little face pops into view so suddenly I can't help but look.

The shorter boy takes advantage of my attention and brings

his cupped hand to his open mouth, the universal sign for food. Beads of sweat run clear tracks through the black grime on his face, an effect of standing in the wake of car exhaust all day.

"I am sorry, I have nothing," I say. "Next time." For emphasis, I open my purse and show them that it is empty. My wallet, of course, is in my pants pocket. I make eye contact with the taller boy and behind the dull expression on his face, I see the bright eyes of a child, dancing with wonder at the sight of three strange women.

I smile and he smiles back. I stick out my tongue and cross my eyes and he starts laughing. The younger boy is startled and steps back from the window, knocking the tall boy's arm from its resting place. As the tall boy moves to put his hand back on the roof, he pauses. He presses his hand against the window, palm splayed and fingers open.

I hear the engine of the taxi rev and the gears shift. In a moment, I will be relieved of the burden of deciding how I can best help these boys: to give or not to give.

I look the boy in the eyes again and put my open hand against his. The warmth of his hand makes its way through the glass. In one last-ditch attempt he rattles the few coins he has in his begging can.

I think about the endeavor Ling Ling, Natalie, and I started at lunch today, our goal of helping poor kids access education.

"Next time," I say. "I will help you if I can in the future."

I am determined to keep my promise.

CHAPTER 15

Visiting L'Ecole Primaire de Point E

I can't wait to get to the school. I envision the energy and color of an elementary school and know it will fuel our excitement. Ling Ling's French teacher, Dienaba, has arranged for us to visit *L'Ecole Primaire de Point E*, and we are following the crude directions through the neighborhood. Point E originally served as housing for the occupying French military and government officials, and the houses are large colonials now owned by the well-educated professionals: the rich Dakaroise. Many of the students who attend *L'Ecole Primaire de Point E* do not come from the immediate neighborhood, but rather from poorer areas on the outskirts of town, walking much farther than we are walking today.

Natalie, Ling Ling and I weave through several mostly residential blocks until we turn a corner and see the school. A cement wall, about eight feet tall and painted white, fences it in. The entrance is two cast-iron gates. Through the gates we can see groups of students standing around, some with backpacks slung over their shoulders, talking and laughing before class. In a matter of seconds, the first student sees us approaching and tells the kids standing around him, who tell the kids standing around them, who tell the kids who eventually tell the whole playground. In a matter of moments, they are all looking at us.

As we search for a doorbell near the gate, a tall man wearing a light yellow tunic and matching pants arrives on the other side. He stands quietly for a moment, just smiling at us, until he finally talks.

"Welcome," he says. "Please come in and meet our school."

As each of us passes him, he introduces himself as Monsieur Sane and extends his right hand, which is covered with white chalk dust. He shakes our hands and leads us into the schoolyard.

The schoolyard is a sandy rectangle bordered on three sides by a two-story building, painted in two solid horizontal blue and white stripes. There are shrubs planted along the edges of the schoolyard, and in one corner there are two full-grown trees, offering shade to several students who stand underneath them.

Monsieur Sane walks us slowly to the main office, pointing out which buildings house which classes. Most of the students have lost interest in us and have gone back to playing in the school yard. One boy chases a group of others in a game of tag, targeting a small fellow whose backpack swaggers side to side as he runs away.

A teacher comes out of the classroom and shouts to the dozens of children straggled over the courtyard. Without hesitation, nearly all of the children turn towards her to listen. When she is finished talking, they walk over to her and begin forming single-file lines. A few of the younger boys who were playing tag hesitate to cut short their fun and linger on the far side of the playground, looking at their feet and tracing lines in the sand. An older boy turns back to them, shouts something, and waits for them to begin walking. When they do, the older boy turns back around and jogs to get in line.

"It's time to take attendance," Monsieur Sane explains to Natalie, Ling Ling and me. The three of us have stopped walking and watch with mouths agape at the display of such discipline among children.

The kids chatter in a mix of Wolof and French. Since the French colonized Senegal and even after independence, the language of instruction in all formal education has been French. As a sign of respect, students call their elders Madame, Mademoiselle, or Monsieur. Outside of the walls of academia, these children address their elders in Wolof with familial titles: Brother, Sister, Uncle, or Aunt, depending on their age.

Monsieur Sane ushers us down the hall into the principal's office where he says we will meet Madame Ndiaye. An immaculately dressed woman bounces up from the chair behind her desk and smiles broadly. The bracelets on her wrists jingle as she walks towards us with her hands clasped together under her chin.

"Welcome," she says. "You must be the students of Dienaba. She is a good friend, and I am happy she sent you to me." She opens her arms broadly and for a moment, I think she is going to engulf Ling Ling in the fabric folds of her bright blue booboo. She stops short and instead thrusts her two hands forward and clasps Ling Ling's hand with them.

We each introduce ourself and sit down in the three chairs Monsieur Sane has carried in from a nearby classroom. When I sit down, I feel a little light-headed. The midmorning heat on our walk to the school wasn't intolerable, but I haven't eaten anything today and it's nearly lunchtime. The combination of hunger, heat, and Madame Ndiaye's energetic enthusiasm have tired me out. I am happy that we already decided that Natalie, whose French is the best among the three of us, will be the designated speaker.

"*Merci*," starts Natalie. "It is a pleasure to be here." She goes on to explain that we want to raise money for students in need and asks if the school will consider partnering with us. We plan on sending a letter to our friends and family, but have no idea how much money it will raise. We are hoping to get an idea of what kind of difference our money could make.

Madame Ndiaye begins speaking, but in a cadence so fast that I cannot follow. I just don't have it in me to follow and translate the conversation. I revert to a trusted bluff—nodding my head when she speaks, aping the replies of Ling Ling and Natalie, and jotting down notes during the silent pauses. I catch the gist of the conversation from Natalie's questions and responses, so I'll just have her and Ling Ling explain the details to me later.

After twenty minutes or so, I can tell Natalie is reviewing what they talked about.

"So the greatest needs are basic," she says. "Uniforms, tuition, books, and supplies."

"I certainly think we can use our money to help students acquire those things," Ling Ling says. "We'll be back in touch when we know how much money we have raised. We are sending out the letter to our friends and families sometime soon."

"*Inshallah*," I say, making Madame Ndiaye smile. Hopefully that is enough to cover my previous ineptitude in the conversation. As we stand up to leave the office and continue our tour with Monsieur Sane, my stomach growls. Our meeting has gone longer than I thought; it must be close to lunch time.

"Do most of the students eat lunch at school?" I ask.

"No, most of our students go home and eat with their families," Madame Ndiaye says. "Some will bring pocket money to buy a sandwich at a nearby boutique."

"You said many of your students do not live in this neighborhood," says Ling Ling. "Do they get back in time for afternoon classes?"

"Some do," Madame Ndiaye responds. "Some come back late and others don't come back at all. Their families can't afford bus fare. Some may not even eat lunch because their family can't afford it. I know these students because if they do return, they are tired and have trouble concentrating in the afternoon. When I can, I give them some pocket change to buy lunch."

"Maybe we should add emergency lunches to our list," says Ling Ling.

"Great idea," says Natalie. She thanks Madame Ndiaye and follows the rest of us out of the office, back onto the open corridor leading to classrooms.

Monsieur Sane is a proud guide, insisting on showing us a classroom before we leave. As we step into the classroom, the teacher stops her lesson. The students are all about eleven years old, some of them gawky teens with acne and others still cherub-faced children. From the looks of the equations written on the blackboard, we've interrupted their math class.

The kids talk excitedly in hushed voices to one another.

"Say '*bonjour*' to the visitors," instructs the teacher. They respond collectively with a loud "*Bonjour!*" The teacher continues. "They are here from the United States. Who knows the United States?"

Nearly all of the students' hands shoot into the air. One boy in the back stands up, so eager to be recognized that he starts jumping up and down.

"Who knows a city in the United States?" the teacher asks the group. A girl wearing a shimmering black shirt drops her hand and turns her head to the side. A wave of green and red beads, each tied to the end of a braid, follows. She smiles at the girl next to her, who is shyly hiding behind her raised arm. The teacher calls on one of the remaining students with his hand raised.

"New York," the boy answers proudly. He tries in vain to mask his smile, which is slowly sprouting on his face.

The students impress us with geopolitical knowledge of our country that would elude most of the interviewees on Jay Leno's "Jay Walking." The name of our president and first lady. The name of their predecessors. A few words in English.

Then the tables are turned on us. "Ask them anything you want," the teacher tells the students, who then look around at each other nervously. One by one the students become brave enough to voice their questions.

"Are you rich?"

"Is it true that every family in America owns a car?"

"Do you all carry guns?"

They sit quietly with wide eyes as we answer. No, we are not rich, but each of our families owns at least one car. I omit that my family of five owns five cars. The three of us laugh out loud at the idea of packing heat, but then see the terror on their faces when we tell them only police officers and people with permits can get guns. The students sit back in their chairs, guarded and skeptical. It takes a few of the classic Senegalese questions before they warm up to us.

"Are you married?"

"How big is your family?"

"Do you have children?"

They laugh when Natalie tells them, in Wolof, that she is looking for a Senegalese husband. When Ling Ling tells them she is married to one *toubab* and one Senegalese husband, but is searching for a third, a skinny boy in the back of the room clutches the edges of the table to keep from falling out of his seat with laughter. They are patient as we try and remember the correct Wolof words for family members and ages, and they smile broadly when I answer them with my flawed French.

At the invitation of the teachers, we walk around the classroom to look at each student's work. They all ask us questions at the same time, tugging at our sleeves to get our individual attention. A girl with eyes as round as buttons gets a firm grip on my wrist and shows off her notebook to me, paging through it so quickly that one page tears slightly.

Eventually, Monsieur Sane thanks the students and reminds them to study hard to make us proud. I look out at them with a smile and see it reflected back on the dozens of little faces before me. Their eagerness is palpable, their will to learn the pulse of the classroom. My own heart swells and I am overcome with the urge to bend down and lift up the girl next to me, to show her how high she is capable of going. I resist, but vow to do what I can to lift these children up, to help lay a solid foundation in education that they can grow on.

The students get back to work copying notes off the blackboard and Monsieur Sane calls the teacher over to talk with us for a minute. I look around at the classroom and, without the noise and movement of the eager students, I notice how bare it is. The walls are painted white and, with the exception of a map of Senegal, there are none of the bright colors and decorations that characterize an elementary classroom back home. No artwork, no posters, no alphabet letter caricatures; nothing but bare walls.

The students are the color in the classroom. A boy with a denim jacket, the sleeves rolled up to his elbows, taps a blue Bic pen on the wooden desk as his eyes wander out the window in thought. Pairs of brown eyes, full of curiosity and light, focus on chalk slates with yellow plastic frames. Notebooks are opened to pages with big cursive letters, drawn in black ink by the steady hands of students. The students sit in groups of three, whispering and laughing when they think no one is looking. It only takes a glance from the teacher to make them hang their heads low, trying to keep their mouths stretched tight over the guilty smiles.

Monsieur Sane explains to the teacher why we are here and asks what the greatest needs of her students are.

"Three students share each textbook," she says. "Sometimes as they huddle together to copy from it, they start chatting and lose concentration. It would be nice if they each had their own."

We thank the teacher, say good-bye to the students, and head out to continue the tour. We walk to the second level of the school to the library, a vast room with a single computer and about 500 books spread out on the floor, which Monsieur Sane explains are being organized and cataloged.

From the balcony outside the library, we have a bird's eye view of the schoolyard, and something becomes clear that I could not see from down below. Etched into the sand are the lines of a soccer field—a large rectangle with a halfway line and a center circle. At either end of the field are lines drawn for the goal, goal area, penalty area, and penalty arc. The detail is enough to impress any soccer enthusiast, but the marks of amateurs are unmistakable: the two goals boxes aren't parallel and one is about ten square feet larger than the other. We are certainly among children: a strong will to play and a foggy grasp on angles.

We leave the school with a new energy. There is so much potential, and the school staff has been so supportive. The three of us all begin talking at once, sharing ideas, enthusiasm, and observations about the school.

"Ladies," I interrupt. "I don't know about you, but I'm starving. LGM is pretty close—does anyone else agree we will think better and be better able to go over the final edits of our letter over pizza?"

Natalie and Ling Ling nod.

"After all," says Natalie. "Like the Senegalese say, *ndank, ndank.* Sometimes, the next step involves eating a good lunch for brain power."

CHAPTER 16

An Answer

Y ou first, Katie," Natalie says. She is bouncing slightly up and down in her chair in the courtyard at the Baobab Center.

It's the morning of our first classes after returning from the holiday break, and when we all ran into each other this morning, we were anxious to get news from one another about how well we've been doing in getting donations from our friends and family. We each sent an email explaining that we would like to help the local elementary school in as many ways as we could, highlighting the needs that Madame Ndiaye, Monsieur Sane, and the other staff at the school had shared with us. Writing the letter, I struggled to keep things honest without relying on the stereotype of Africa as full of despair. I pulled from my background writing grants, stuck to concrete data to make my point, and came up with this:

> *Through our first-hand experience in Senegal, we have seen the devastating constraints of a country where 73% of the population is illiterate. There is no lack of potential causes for this alarming rate: classes average 65 students, teaching supplies are limited and outdated, and one tattered textbook is usually shared among three students. In addition, there are a number of students who come from families that are too poor to feed them lunch. Therefore, in the afternoon, they either return too hungry to concentrate, or do not return at all. We thought that if we could raise some money it could be used to*

make small purchases that would have big effects on student retention rates: notebooks, uniforms, emergency lunches, and other school essentials.

I am writing you today to ask for your help. We have partnered with a local primary school that will use any money that we raise to address the needs of their poorest students. This Christmas, I ask that you help support our efforts by making a small gift to our project. A gift of any amount can make a huge difference.

"I have to say," I start, "I hate asking people for money, but it turns out they don't hate giving it as much. I have almost $800."

"Ling Ling?" Natalie asks.

"Well, it turns out my friends and family have the ño ko bokk spirit too," Ling Ling answers. "I have collected $1,400."

"Oh my goodness, praise God!" Natalie exclaims. She puts the palms of both her hands to her forehead, fingers splayed. "That means with the gifts I received, we have raised over $3,000!"

We are all silent for a minute, letting it sink in. I remembered the day on the beach, when our idea was born with a question from Natalie. *How many students can we help?*

"This is going to help more students than we could have dreamed of," I say.

CHAPTER 17

A Dakar Reunion, A Dakar Good-bye

I roll over to grab my cell phone on the bedside table in a confused state. It's not even 7:00 a.m. yet, meaning it must be either someone who doesn't know me that well or who is calling from a different time zone. I answer it anyway.

"Ahlo?" I say, my voice gruffy with an exaggerated French accent.

"Katie!" Mariama says on the other end of the phone. It's been weeks since I last saw her, but I recognize her voice instantly. I remember my last meeting with the teenager, her son Babu wrapped in a blanket on her back and an empty bucket in her hand. She'd come to the *campement* to tell her father Musa that lunch was ready, and to fill up the bucket with water from the well for washing dishes. Her chubby cheeks sat like plump crabapples at the ends of her bright smile when she waved and said hello.

"Mariama!" I say. "How are you…?" I want to add "…calling me?" since I know that making a phone call from Yayeme is a challenge. She would either have to chance upon someone with a charged cell phone (unlikely in a village with no electricity) or walk twenty minutes from Yayeme to Fimela—the closest village with electricity.

"Katie, I can't talk long, I don't have many minutes left," says Mariama. "I am in Dakar."

"You are?" I say. "That's great! Where can I meet you?"

"I am staying with my uncle in Niaritali. Do you know that part of town?"

"No. What is your uncle's address?"

"I don't know," Mariama says. "But I need to see you. I have something for you."

"Are you near the University?" I ask, trying to think of a central place that is easily recognizable. I hear Mariama ask someone in the room with her and hear several people respond.

"Yes," she says finally. "My uncle knows the University."

"Can you meet this afternoon at the University's library?" I ask. Again, I hear her conference with the people around her.

"Yes," she says. "This afternoon is good."

"I'll be there around 4:00," I say, knowing that means next to nothing to her, a visitor from the countryside where morning, afternoon, and night are as specific as time ever gets. "I'll wait for you outside the library."

"A bientôt," Mariama says. Before I can respond, our connection is cut off, her pre-paid credit having finally run out.

* * *

It has been weeks since I returned to Dakar from Yayeme. The sharp longing to return to Yayeme has not subsided, but I've fallen back into my routine in Dakar. Class. Writing stories and doodling in my journal. Visiting friends. I've tried to embody the charm of Yayeme that I miss most—not thinking it odd to stop to talk with a friend for thirty minutes after a chance encounter on the street; accepting dinner invitations from near-strangers; believing that each day is predestined, or at least strongly influenced by God's will, and learning to go with the flow.

When I got back to Dakar I had to pick up some clothes from the tailor, which proved to be the first test of my new, relaxed state. It was days after the tailor told me my clothes would be ready, and when I poked my head in the door of her shop, she smiled from behind the manual sewing machine. Her foot was pedaling to spin the rubber belt that powered the machine. She told me she hadn't started mending my skirts yet because things came up. Rather than threaten her with the idea of taking my business elsewhere, I asked about her family and accepted an invitation to stay for tea. By the time I left, the afternoon had been so pleasant that I barely remembered the unfinished alterations.

I missed my friends from Yayeme. I missed Diène. I thought how proud they would be of my laid-back attitude and efforts to enjoy each day and the people around me. I wished that there was a reliable way to call them, remembering our so-far broken promises to keep in touch. This is why I have been answering all my calls lately, even the early morning ones.

I lie in bed for a while, thinking of the day ahead. Natalie, Ling Ling, and I are going to visit *L'Ecole Primaire de Point E*. After we told the school how much money we had raised, we were able to have a frank discussion on how to best use the gifts. It turns out that one of the most pressing needs at the school is also one of the most basic. Hunger. During our meetings with Madame Ndiaye and Monsieur Sane we went over the numbers and discovered that hiring a cook, stocking the kitchen with supplies, and buying ingredients for basic lunches was more economical than giving out emergency lunch stipends on a one-on-one basis.

The only thing we couldn't afford to do was build a decent kitchen, but with typical Senegalese faith, Madame Ndiaye was confident that if we started with a cook and gas burner in the back of the school yard, things would work out for the best. Today, we are going to the school for the last time as a threesome; Ling Ling's time in Dakar is coming to a close, and she'll be leaving for home in a few days.

"Madame Ndiaye has some news for us," says Ling Ling on our walk to the school. "She didn't go into detail on the phone, but she said it was really important."

Monsieur Sane greets us at the door and ushers us into Madame Ndiaye's office. I feel infinitely more equipped to participate in this discussion than I did at our first meeting. Traveling alone and being forced to speak only French and Wolof for nearly two weeks has brought me to a new level of comprehension in both.

Madame Ndiaye looks up from a stack of paperwork on her desk and smiles broadly.

"Hello, hello!" she says. "How are my friends today?" She walks over to us and puts her arm around Natalie's shoulder, slightly pulling her towards the door. "Come with me, I want to show you something."

We exit her office and instead of turning left towards the classrooms, we walk to the right, towards the far corner of the property where there is nothing but a pile of broken cinderblocks stacked next to a hastily build canopy of thatched leaves standing above a tank of propane gas and a single gas burner. There is a woman sitting on a wooden stool next to the gas tank, chopping onions and throwing them into the pan. Each morsel sizzles when it hits the hot oil in the bottom of the pan.

"This is Fatou," says Madame Ndiaye. "Our cook." The woman tosses the onion pieces from her hand into the pan, grabs the hem of her faded multicolored booboo to wipe her sweaty brow, and then greets us.

"From this small kitchen, Fatou makes twenty-one separate bowls of *ceeb bu jeen* (fish and rice) or *yassa poulet* (chicken and onion sauce) twice a week for the lunch program." Madame Ndiaye is practically shouting, but it is difficult to hear her because there is some heavy-duty construction work on the other side of the wall. Men are shouting and a truck engine is sputtering.

"You hear that?" asks Madame Ndiaye. "The company that is building the house next door has disrupted our class several times with their work noise. The students have gotten used to it, but as a gesture of goodwill, they have offered to build us a kitchen."

"A kitchen?" Ling Ling asks.

"Yes, a kitchen," says Madame Ndiaye. She pauses a moment. "For free."

"For free!?" the three of us exclaim simultaneously. Fatou looks up at us, and without stopping her chopping, smiles broadly.

"What is the proverb Zator taught us in class?" asks Natalie. *"Man plans, God decides."*

Madame Ndiaye laughs with delight and walks us to her office. "Stay and watch the children eat lunch," she says. "You will see what your work has done."

We peek inside a fourth-grade classroom where two groups of about ten students each are circled around a common bowl, each with a hunk of bread in their left hand and a spoon in their right. They eat mostly without talking. One boy takes a piece of meat from the center of the bowl, cuts off a small morsel into the rice directly in front of him and then places the remainder in the center of the bowl. He grunts, his mouth full, urging the others to enjoy the piece of meat he's cut for them.

We know that if the students see us, they will get up to say hello and we don't want to disturb their lunch so we sneak away unseen. Outside of the school, we linger in conversation about what our next steps in the project should be.

"I know I am leaving," says Ling Ling. "But I'd like to keep working on the school lunch project." She looks at Natalie and me with determined eyes. "I think we could continue to do good work from home. All of us, if we stay committed."

"I'm in," I say. I haven't decided yet exactly when I will be going home, but my French and Wolof classes are drawing to a close. The project seems like a natural way to stay connected to Senegal once I have to leave.

Natalie nods in agreement. "Me, too," she says. "What do you think we can do from home to be the most useful?"

"Talk to people about our work," says Ling Ling. "Let them know how they can help, if they are interested."

"We'll stay in touch with the school," says Natalie, "and be sure that things are progressing here, too. If the new kitchen is any sign of things to come, this could become a very interesting partnership."

"I can't believe it's almost over," I say. "The three of us here in Dakar together." I look at my two friends standing in front of me, the sun shining in their squinting eyes and the closed iron gate of the school at their backs. Next to us, a group of dusty construction workers stand around a large pile of cinderblocks, debating what to do next. Down the block, a graying old man sits in a plastic chair in the shade of a juniper tree, smoking a cigarette and watching us from afar. I want to grab this moment, this scene, and keep it this vivid in my mind forever.

"This is only the beginning," says Ling Ling.

* * *

As I walk to the University, I ponder our good fortune. First our friends and family give the school enough money for us to help build an entire lunch program. Our project starts with meager, humble beginnings and good intentions and sure enough, a group of strangers offers to build a kitchen. Those kids eating! I don't feel like I am actually doing anything to help them, but rather simply being a conduit of others' goodwill. I feel so grateful for the opportunity that when a group of *talibé* start following me, I give them all the change I have in my pocket, telling them to split it up evenly.

I arrive at the University for my 4:00 meeting with Mariama, and my cell phone shows me it is 4:20. I know Mariama isn't here yet; if she had arrived before me she would wait. I find an empty bench in a shady part of the library's courtyard and settle in to wait. Across from me, there is a photographer taking portraits of students. Behind him, a line of waiting students has formed in the shade. The students are dressed up in trendy fashion clothes and chat with each other while waiting for their turn. A beautiful woman is posing for the camera with her hands on her hips and her zigzag braids thrown back. The photographer snaps a few shots and then gestures for her to move a few feet to her right, putting a lovely green bush with fiery yellow flowers in the background of the frame. The camera looks like one that my dad has on the top shelf of his closet that he only takes down when he's feeling reminiscent; the flash bulb is nearly as big as the lens itself.

After the next five people make it through the photo line and I grow tired of watching them, I look at my cell phone. 5:15. I no longer get annoyed at the inevitable tardiness of everyone working on Senegalese time, but I still don't understand how to make it work for me. I always seem to be the one waiting for hours. My only defense is to always carry a book.

I pull out my copy of Tanya Shaffer's *Somebody's Heart is Burning: A Woman Wanderer in Africa*. It's a story of a young woman's travels around Africa, and almost each time I finish a chapter, I compulsively flip to the "About the Author" section. I am searching for something that reassures me I could do the same thing, a spark for my dream to write a book and sell hundreds of thousands of copies.

Finally, my cell phone shows 6:15 and I know, even on Senegalese time, Mariama is not coming.

I scroll through the calls-received log on my phone and dial the number that Mariama called me from this morning.

"Ahlo?" I hear a man say.

"Hello," I say. "Is Mariama there?"

"Mariama?" he asks. I can hear lots of voices in the background and realize I'm calling a telecenter.

"Mariama Marie Mbaye," I say. "She is visiting her uncle, Modou Mbaye."

"Yes, yes! Modou!" says the guy on the other end. "I know him."

"Mariama is his niece. I think she came in to make a call this morning."

"Yes, yes," says the guy. "Call back in ten minutes. I will send my son to go get her."

I wait twenty minutes and call back.

"Katie?" says Mariama. "Listen, I wanted to call you and tell you that I can't make it to the University today. I don't have any money for the cab ride."

"No problem," I say, trying not to be slightly annoyed. Didn't she think of that before we made plans this morning? I stand up from where I've been sitting and start walking home while talking to her on the phone.

"Can you come visit tomorrow morning?" she asks. "The wedding begins after lunch. Maybe you could come before then." I don't respond before she says, "I have something important for you. Diène sent it."

"OK," I say. Bribery seems to work. "Where do I take the taxi?"

"Just tell your driver to come to the big field in Niaritali. I'll wait for you there."

I do as I am told the next morning, and am shocked that the taxi driver seems to know exactly what the "big field in Niaritali" means. We drive to a part of town I have never seen before where the buildings are five stories of cramped apartments, with laundry hanging from the open windows and children playing in the dusty patches between their front doors and the street. The traffic is congested and moves slowly; when we stall at a red light, a scooter behind us hops the curb and drives on the sidewalk, weaving between pedestrians and children playing. I hold my breath while the puny red scooter bounces along the cracks in the pavement, its course shifting in directions the driver seems unable to control. Two blocks later, the driver reaches the intersection and drives over the curb into the traffic, and I exhale.

The taxi stops and lets me out in front of a wide, open patch of dust. I see kids playing soccer, merchants hawking their goods, groups of *talibé* loitering together, a pair of old men chatting and smoking cigarettes, and Mariama walking towards me.

"Mariama!" I say, giving her a big hug. I say "hi" to Babu, who is wrapped on her back. She leads me to her uncle's house, through narrow alleys between the tall apartment buildings. At one steel gate, indecipherable from the rest, we turn and go in.

We enter a small landing below two staircases on either side of the building. Just past the staircases, a little boy is crouched by a faucet, filling a bucket with water. We climb up three flights of stairs and walk down a narrow hallway with one side open, overlooking the open landing. Sheets are hung over the side of the walls to dry. We enter a small room where a group of girls are getting ready for the wedding. One is braiding her sister's hair, and another one is putting on eyeshadow using a small compact mirror. Two of the youngest are trying on the shoes of all their older cousins and attempting to walk around the room in high heels. The room is modest and unadorned except for a single bed and dresser and a lacy white tapestry hanging behind the bed.

Mariama introduces me to everyone and immediately the woman who is braiding hair stands up out of her chair and nudges the woman whose hair she was braiding. They move to the bed, insisting I sit in the chair.

"Oh, no. It's okay," I say, knowing I will not win this battle. I sit down.

Mariama asks me how I've been, if I have any news from my family, and how my writing and school have been going.

"I almost forgot!" she says, at one point. "Diène sent you something." She leaves for a minute and then returns lugging a heavy, plastic bag.

I untie the top of the plastic bag and peer in. Inside are about 40 yellow grapefruits. I pick the bag up to try and count them, only to set it back down as I realize how heavy it is.

"Mariama! I can't believe you carried this the whole trip." I imagine the cramped bus ride, and try not to imagine where on the bus my bag of fruit was stowed.

"I held them," she says, reading my mind. "Diène is a good friend of mine. He is a kind person. He would've rather given them to you himself, but since he can't, I told him I would." The youngest girl on the bed whispers something to her pal and all the girls giggle.

Mariama is bouncing Babu on her knee, while a clear line of snot drips down his chin. Mariama wipes his face clean and whispers something to him. He is fussy, arching his back and trying to get out of Mariama's grip. In the company of her "city" cousins, I see Mariama from a different perspective. She is one of the youngest of her adult cousins and the only one with a child.

The cousin who was putting on the eyeshadow has finished and offers to take Babu. She grabs him from Mariama's arms and motions for her to take the eyeshadow. While Mariama opens up the compact, Babu starts whining and the cousin takes him out of the room. I am astonished when she exits out of the lacy curtain hung behind the bed; it was serving not as a decoration but as a wall, dividing a small room into two in this cramped apartment.

For a while, the girls talk, excited about the wedding. They give me the skinny on the bride, whom she is marrying, and how she is related to everyone. After about an hour, an older woman comes in, with Babu in her arms, and tells the girls it's time to go.

"I'll walk you to find a taxi," says Mariama. She wipes Babu's snotty nose and gives him a kiss on the forehead before she walks me out and back to the big field.

My arm is tired from carrying the heavy bag of grapefruits for a few blocks, and I am anxious to take a load off in the back of a cab.

As we say our good-byes, Mariama looks at her feet, kicking around the dust. I wonder if I've done something to offend her. Finally, as I wave a taxi over, Mariama speaks.

"Katie, I have a problem," she blurts out.

"What is it, Mariama?" I ask. "Is everything okay?"

"I need to go back to Yayeme tomorrow, but I don't have any money for the bus fare."

"I can give you money, Mariama," I say. Almost instantly, I regret how quickly I offered. Like I couldn't wait to get rid of her.

"No, no," she says. "That is too nice. I just don't know what to do. I had enough money when I arrived, but then Babu got sick and I had to buy some medicine. He is not used to the city or the dust on the bus. I still had enough to get back, but then all my cousins and sisters were pooling their money to give to the bride.

I had to participate—it's not right to come to someone's wedding without giving them a gift."

"Mariama," I say. "I can give you the money. It's no big deal."

"Yes it is, Katie," she says. "I wanted to come give you the grape-fruits yesterday, but now you understand why I couldn't. I just wanted you to know."

I pull a few thousand CFA out of my wallet and hand them to Mariama. Her hands are folded together in front of her, and she holds them up to refuse.

"No, Katie. It's fine. I just wanted to tell you."

"Mariama," I say. "It's not for you." She looks up at me, a bit surprised.

"It's for Babu. I want to make sure he stays healthy while he is here and that he can get home safely. I know he must be tired from the trip." The bags under her eyes tell me he is not the only one.

"Thank you," she says and takes the money from my hands. "Thank you for Babu, and God bless you."

We hug good-bye.

"I'll miss you," I say.

"I am sure I will see you again soon," she says.

"*Inshallah*," we both say at the same time, and then we laugh.

LESSON 6

Faydah
A sense of self
Wolof

Lu bant yàgg-yàgg ci ndox,
du tax mu soppaliku mukk jasig
Even if a log soaks a long time in water,
it will never become a crocodile
Wolof Proverb

Even in a communal society, there must be room for individuals to express themselves and their unique personalities. Faydah is the strength to know who you are and to use your gifts to benefit the community. Natalie, Ling Ling, and I each brought very different personalities and strengths to the work of Project Japalé Gouné, and the greatest gift Senegal gave me was the time and space to discover my own faydah.

CHAPTER 18

The First Rain

I am taking deeper breaths. Cherishing more moments. Lingering longer in salutations. I have picked the date I will fly back home to the United States; I have begun saying my good-byes to Senegal. I now have to take it all in as much as I can, because soon it will be gone. Most days I am excited to see my friends and family back home. When I talked to my mom on the phone to tell her I was coming home, I could nearly feel my heart beating its way out of my chest.

Other days I wonder if I should try to stretch out my budget and stay after my classes have ended, to maximize my time here. On these days I have Diène and Yayeme on my mind, the hardest part of my journey to leave behind. The one part of Senegal I am not sure I can leave behind forever.

My sooner-than-expected departure has busied me with last visits to favorite places, trips to buy souvenirs, and attempts to do all the things I feel I can't leave Senegal without doing. Yet, every day I go to the *le cyber*, a place of routine that has become comfortable, a home away from home.

Purvi, another Rotary Scholar and good friend, is reading emails in the otherwise empty *cyber* when I arrive.

"Hey, Katie!" she says, with her characteristic broad smile. "Check out this writing contest that some guy in California is sponsoring. I am going to forward the email to you."

A moment later, the message is in my in-box and I read the rules of a travel writing contest.

Attention Backpackers: Have you traveled to the developing world and met an individual, family, organization, or village that shared something with you? Can you think of a way they may use $1,000? Enter the Backpack Nation writing contest and win $1,000 to share with the people you've met in your travels. Send stories about your projects, lessons learned, and how you intend to share the money with people you have met during your travels. The five best stories will be awarded a $1,000 prize.

"Oh, Purvi, how cool!" I say. "Are you thinking of entering?"

"No. You!" she says. "I think you should enter. You should write about Yayeme."

"Hmm," I say. "I am leaving later this week for one last Yayeme visit—it could be a good time to pick up some inspiration." My mind is already spinning with opening lines and descriptive details. "I don't know, though—I have so much to do before I go back home."

"Katie," Purvi says. "It seems like the only thing you've been doing since you got back from Yayeme is writing about it! How hard can it be to turn those stories into an entry for this contest? Don't chicken out."

I turn my head back to the computer, and I know she is right. I read over the guidelines online, jot a few notes down in my notebook, and then go on to my next email.

"All right," I say. "I guess I'll just add it to the list of things to do."

I don't think of the contest again for almost another week, until I am lying in bed in a hut in Yayeme, under the cover of my mosquito net. It is my last night, and tomorrow I will say good-bye to everyone for what could be the last time. I can't sleep, and every time I drift off, a loud thump on the ceiling of my hut startles me awake. The last of the season's overripe mangoes are falling from the tree above my hut, most likely with the aid of the nibbling fruit bats, and when they land on the soft thatch of the roof, they roll to the edge and then fall to the ground with a plunk. This brings the contest to mind. This detail of falling mangoes seems important enough to include in the story somehow. My entire life in Yayeme seems to have taken place in the shade of mango trees.

Tonight, the air in Yayeme is heavy with humidity and anticipation. A neighbor who had returned to Yayeme after a day of travel said that last night there was rain in Fatick, about thirty miles northeast of us. Late in the evening, I sat with Diène, Musa, and Diène's brother, Waly, under the mango tree, and out of the corner of my eye I saw veins of electricity illuminate the night sky in the distance. Musa wondered aloud if he had been smoking too much *cali*, but we laughed and confirmed we had all seen it, too.

We waited for the thunder, which didn't come right away. Musa wanted to hurry home, but I pleaded with him and Waly to stay a little longer; tonight was my last night. We didn't speak of it, but we knew that the year's first rain could be on its way. When we said good-night, we all looked to the sky. For the first time in Yayeme, I could not see the stars.

Now, I think about the story for the contest. How can I capture the sense of community I've found here? How can I show how kind the Senegalese are? How can I illustrate how meaningful the gesture of a shared meal is when many American families no longer eat dinner together as a family? I've spent almost a year searching for Wolof words to express myself, sometimes finding the word I need doesn't exist. Will it be the same when I try to translate Senegalese culture into English?

The wind is growing stronger outside my hut, throwing more mangoes onto my roof. Each one makes me think it's the first of the raindrops, but I smell the rain before I hear it. It's the smell of hot sand and earth drinking in the first refreshment in over eight months. Then I hear the tinkling on the metal roof of the attached bathroom and recognize it as the unmistakable sound of rain. I hear neighbors getting up out of their beds, leaving their huts and standing in the rain. I decide to do the same.

I walk outside, arms outstretched, and let the rain soak me. I feel giddy. Rain, sweet rain. How we appreciate you when you only come three months out of the year. How lucky I am to be here for the first rain of the season!

Diène comes out of his hut, and for a moment we just smile at each other, soaking up the rain. I look over at him and miss him already. I miss the way I want to be nice to everyone when I am around him. I miss the way his face reveals little, yet changes so drastically from moment to moment, the way his eyes dance from mood to mood.

"I am happy I didn't go home before the rain," I say. "What good luck."

"Not luck," he says. "I think it was your *faydah* that gave you the strength to stay in Senegal until the first rain. You must have wanted it."

"*Faydah?*" I ask.

"*Faydah* is knowing yourself, knowing what you want. To feed your family, you must have the *faydah* to work hard in the fields."

I knit my eyebrows together in confusion. "You mean discipline, or motivation?"

"*Faydah* is what makes dreams come true, what lays the path ahead of you as you walk through the forest. It allows you to accept a friend's invitation for tea, it guides you as you treat others with the respect that you deserve for yourself. *Faydah* gives you the courage to take decisive action.

"It is the seed God planted in your heart, and your life is meant to serve its cultivation."

"When I first met you," I say, "you told me everything that is planted in Yayeme grows. Do you think my *faydah* will shrivel when I go back home?"

"*Faydah* grows in the heart," he says. "The heart has no borders or limits, in time or space."

Why does mine ache so painfully, then, as I think of the distance there is about to be put between the two of us?

The next morning, I walk out of my hut to see that the earth has woken up. I drink in the piney musk coming from my damp thatched roof. Outside, the rain has washed the layer of dust off of everything. The leaves of the tress are lacquered with shine and exploding with green. The yard looks brand new, as if I've dusted off an old photo in the attic to find color and detail underneath. Insect eggs have hatched, saturating the air with clusters of tiny bugs, stretching their fledging wings.

For many, the rain has brought a feast. Birds poke their beaks into new holes in the sand, searching for insect clusters. Lizards skedaddle up and down the branches of the tree, chasing the plump insects. I walk to the kitchen for breakfast, and mosquitoes feast on my ankles, making me very aware of my own position in the newly arranged food chain. Near the kitchen door, the earth is covered with fire-red spiders, their blood flowing in translucent skin.

"*Les fils de Dieu,*" Diène tells me as he points to the insects, crawling over one another like a litter of puppies whose eyes haven't opened yet.

Musa comes by while we eat and says he can only stay for a while. For him, the rain has brought work. It exposed a hole in his roof that needs repair. It has hastened planning with his brother about when to clear the fields. It threatens to spoil the livestock's feed that his sons will need to clean up.

As a parting gift, I give Musa my best pen, a retractable gel ink one with a fat silver barrel, soft rubber grip cushion, and a shiny silver clip. Compared to the crappy ballpoint pens for sale in the local boutique, this is a luxury item of great decadence.

"For your horse race calculations," I say.

"A rich pen like this," Musa says, clipping it in his breast pocket, "can only bring me money." Then he extends his left hand. "We shake with our left hand instead of our right because it means we will see you again."

I extend my left hand and smile, wishing him well.

"I wish I could see you off," he says. "But the rain has come. Our period of rest is over. Now the work begins."

Diène insists on accompanying me to Dakar and I am grateful to delay my most dreaded good-bye. On the bus ride, he says he'll visit his aunt, who lives in my neighborhood. That way he can stay until the day of my flight and see me to the airport.

In Dakar, I unlock the door to my apartment and walk into my studio to see everything covered in a layer of orange dust. It did not rain in Dakar, and the city is still dry and thirsty. I had shut the windows and doors, but somehow the sediment managed to creep in anyway. I have only been gone for a long weekend, but it feels like I am entering a long-abandoned homestead.

I pull my huge backpack off and plop it down on the bed, which lifts a layer of dust off the cover and into the air. I open the windows next to my desk and pull my laptop from its case in my closet and sit down at my desk. I only have one day before the contest deadline and a few more before I leave Senegal for good. I have a million things I want to do, but as I sit down to write, I think of what Musa said. My time of rest is over. Now my work begins.

CHAPTER 19

Love

There is something hanging around, a presence that is helping me get through the day. The superstitious of Senegal would tell me it's my ancestors, protecting me on the day of a long journey, but I am not so sure. It isn't until I see a nun sitting in the corner of the airport shuttle bus, her hands folded in the lap of her black habit, a gold cross on a chain around her neck, that I realize what it is. She is probably a missionary, perhaps even one from the Josman health clinic near Yayeme, who has finished her service to the people of Senegal and is returning home. Behind her serenity, behind her peaceful smile, there is something familiar.

The day was a whirlwind of activity, and Diène and I didn't have more than twenty minutes of time alone. This morning I ran last-minute errands, nervous I didn't have the right souvenirs and gifts for family back home. In the afternoon, friends came over to say good-bye and wish me *"bon voyage."* When evening came and it was time to catch a taxi to the airport, Diène and I said good-bye to the neighbors Diène had befriended during his visits in the last week. I hugged the mother, a fat woman who had entertained us all evening with tales of her trip to the United States to visit her son, where she gained twenty pounds in three months. When Diène and she hugged good-bye, he sort of collapsed in her arms, and buried his teary face in her shoulder. A mother of twelve children, she knew what to do, and let him cry until he was ready to stop. As we walked out, she pulled me aside.

"That boy has the spirit of an angel," she said. "Don't forget that the burden of pain rests with the one who is left behind."

At the airport, Diène and I didn't have much to say. Every time I began to speak, I got too choked up to continue. I felt conspicuous, wearing my travel clothes and standing among my luggage in the crowded airport next to Diène in his jeans, T-shirt, and flip-flops. I hated how obvious it was that only one of us was leaving.

Our last moment was a tight, long hug with promises to reunite by phone and in person as soon, and as often, as we could. When it was finally time, I turned and got in line for security without looking back. I could feel Diène's gaze on me, but I was afraid that if I turned around, my knees would weaken and my body would grow immobile. If I turned around to look back, I was afraid I wouldn't be able to move forward.

Now I am crammed in the crowded airport shuttle bus, with all the other New York-bound passengers. An American family is talking loudly next to me about the things they are afraid of going back to, the things they know will be difficult to face. "We just have so much we take for granted," says the father, who accidently knocks into the seated nun as he shifts his weight.

I watch her modestly recross her feet to make more room for the man, not a trace of resentment in her aura. She catches my eye and smiles at me with a face full of tranquility, fingering the cross at her neck. I recognize the peace and calm emanating from her, the thing that lights up her face. It's the same thing I saw in Brigitte's face, the day she caught me with melted cookie all over my face. It's what led Pop, Amse, and me to retrace our steps through Marchè Sandaga. It's in Ibu's devotion to Baye Fall, and what made it so easy for him to learn English from Bob Marley. It's in Astou's daily service to her husband, ten children, and extended family. It's what the Senegalese shine on one another, through bright smiles and kind words. It's the money that my friends and family sent in response to my letter about our neighborhood school kids in need. It's each word of the story I entered into the travel writing contest. It's what is wrapped tightly around my heart now, constricting my chest and making it hard to breathe. It's the last thing I expected to find in Senegal, and the thing that now makes it so difficult to leave.

It is love.

CHAPTER 20

Land of the Lonely

It's always hard for me not to giggle during the singing. I know it's immature, but it's the same feeling I get in church when the very last thing I should be doing is laughing. I am sitting in a breakfast meeting of the Mayfair Rotary club, with the Rotarians who sponsored my year in Senegal. I've been to enough meetings to know that after the singing comes the "Happy Fines" and that is my favorite part. Members of the club pay to share good news, and all the money collected goes to a charity of the club's choice. Singing, healthy breakfast, good news, and philanthropy. What a great way to start the day.

When it is my turn to speak, I get up to the podium with a few butterflies in my stomach. I've spent days writing my talk and preparing a slideshow. It is very important to me to show Senegal as more than a poor country; I want my speech to show it as a wise country. As I talk and advance through the photos on the projector, I feel like my friends are there with me. Mariama and Babu. Diène. Mami Chou. All of their faces projected on the screen alleviate my nervousness.

I share some of the things I learned from the Senegalese: hospitality, the sharing spirit, a sense of faith. I talk about our work setting up the lunch program at *L'Ecole Primaire de Point E* and end with a plea for everyone to go online and vote for my story in the Backpack Nation contest: it has made the judges' first cut, and now voting is open to the public.

After my presentation, I take questions, and a man in the back of room raises his hand.

"About the lunch program. How can we help?" he asks.

"How very Senegalese of you to ask," I joke.

Later in the week, I leave my parents' house and head out the back door.

"Bye, guys!" I shout. "I'm off to Starbucks." I hear two good-byes: from my mom reading in the living room and my dad working in the basement. My brother is up in his room playing video games; I didn't really expect to hear from him. The house is full, but I still feel like I am home alone. I expected to indulge in the alone time waiting for me back home in Wisconsin; I never thought it would make me feel so lonely.

I have walked this route thousands of times, from my parents' house to the Village in Wauwatosa, but I feel like I am seeing it for the first time. The perfect green lawns of the massive homes on Warren Avenue, each blade of grass the same length as the next. Such order, such conformity. For most of my walk, I see no one until a woman with a dog on a leash walks towards me. When she passes I instinctively say hello, startling her enough that she quickly snaps her gaze from the sidewalk to me and takes a step back. She looks at me and smiles, but says nothing.

As I crest the small hill, I see an oscillating sprinkler that has been left to water a lawn. Clean, potable water shoots up from the metal bar, making a wall of water. It lands on the lawn for the most part, but overshoots slightly and ends up dampening the concrete of the sidewalk and driveway. I stop and stare at the water running down the sidewalk. In three minutes, I am sure more water has been given to the concrete than could fill my daily shower bucket in Yayeme.

At the end of my walk, I arrive at Starbucks and meet an old friend to catch up over a cup of coffee. After hugs, pleasantries, and ordering our $4 espresso drinks, we sit down to talk.

"So—how was Africa? Tell me everything!" she says.

"Well, Senegal was…" Between us are two espresso drinks and

two bakery items, the money we spent just over $10. I search for the words to describe my trip, and all I can think of is that little boy with the mismatched flip-flops and his family. And how by buying this mid-morning snack, I have kept another family like his naked.

"It was incredible," I finally say. "A totally different world." I shift uncomfortably in my seat. I've had this conversation a number of times since I came back, and it never ends like I want it to.

"What was the most shocking thing for you?" she asks, licking frothy milk from her top lip.

"How differently time moves in Senegal," I say. "And how kind everyone is to one another. Almost every day, a stranger or someone I'd just met invited me over for dinner."

"Ew. Kinda creepy," she says, scrunching up her face. "What did you miss most?"

"Soymilk and dark chocolate," I say, expecting a laugh that doesn't come. "And, uh, my family... of course."

"Hmm," she says. "Did you see any lions?"

I feel like a visitor here, in my hometown, where life is so good. Only minutes from my house, Starbucks offers the luxury of food and drink, overstuffed furniture, and jazz on the stereo. Why can't I shake the feeling I am in a hospital waiting room or some other sterile environment created to keep people's attention off what is really going on just outside of view?

My senses are bored. In Senegal, there would be shouting, loud music—perhaps even competing radios—and the constant blare of honking horns from traffic. The air would be thick with the heat and smells of the city, not a filtered 72 degrees with the sanitized aroma of freshly ground coffee. In Dakar, we'd be sitting on hard, stout wooden stools, not slouching in plush couches.

Maybe the numbing of our senses is what makes it so easy for Americans to live our lives without thinking of the world outside of our own. The comfort we've slipped into in our physical and material environments mirrors the comfort with which we accept our ignorance about the rest of the world. Most of the people I've spoken to about my trip have never heard of Senegal, let alone know where in Africa it is. There is the tendency to lump Africa together as one large pot of despair: AIDS, famine, genocide, and, yes, lions are the first things that come to mind for the majority of Americans when they think of Africa.

I do my best not to hold my friend's ignorant question against her.

"No," I say and quickly change the subject. "What's new with you?"

It feels good to sit with an old friend and connect. We catch up on the progression of our early twenties and wonder out loud if we are doing the right thing, moving in the right direction.

"Well, I should get going," she announces. I stay seated, expecting her departure to be in twenty minutes or so. In Senegal, it was only polite to give such a warning, so I am taken aback when she gets up abruptly. We gather our barely used paper coffee cups, their java jackets, plastic lids, and the extra napkins that came with our pastries, and toss them into the garbage on our way out. I think of the repurposed yellow brake fluid bottle I drank juice from in Yayeme. We talk as we walk out together.

"Now what?" she asks, her keys dangling from her hand as she stands next to her car. "Are you going to stay here in town and look for a job?"

"For the summer, at least. Actually, I'd like to go back to Senegal, if things with the writing contest work out."

"Oh yeah, that's right! I'll vote for you online as soon as I get home today," she says, smiling. "Any idea what will come after that?"

I cringe at the question I dread most. I long for the Senegalese conversations void of questions about plans for the future. Why plan when God has the final say? I miss the discussions that reassured each other of the good things God would bring. While I found the constant wishing of peace on ourselves and our families superficial while I was there, I feel like I could really use the reassurance now. Faith in good things seems a natural first step in getting them.

"To be honest," I start, "I have no idea." I laugh nervously. She just looks at me, her lips pressed together in a flat smile. Then her eyes roll upward and her grin opens up.

"None of us do!" she says. "It's good to hear someone so honest."

I laugh again with relief.

"I guess the only thing I have to do any time soon is get people to vote for my story." That's the first step. *Ndank, ndank.*

* * *

Later that week, I get a phone call from the Rotarian who had taken an interest in the school lunch program.

"It's a funny coincidence," he says. "I've been looking for a way to expand my own giving to impact people in need internationally. Then you speak at our Rotary meeting, talking about exactly what I've been looking for. Anyway, the club has decided to donate half of all of its 'Happy Fines' to the project, and I will match that."

I am smiling on my end of the phone. I can't wait to call Ling Ling and Natalie. "Hopefully," he says, "we'll be able to feed lots of those hungry minds."

CHAPTER 21

Power of the Pen Redux

I am not surprised by the power of the pen in Senegal. After all, it is what has brought me back. When I go through customs, I need not bribe the bureaucrat; the two most important gifts I will be sharing are not something I have in my suitcase. After I find my luggage on the carousel, I leave the airport and get a taxi into Dakar.

The capital is exploding with life. Green erupts from every patch of soil, even the medians and shoulders of the roads, which I always saw as dusty voids with little use other than makeshift marketplaces for unlucky goats before any big holiday that involved feasting. In the two months that I have been gone, the rainy season has nourished the city. Drop by drop, the urban expanse has transformed from a sandy expanse of concrete and car exhaust to an area bursting with fresh life.

I have only one thing to take care of in Dakar before I leave for Yayeme. Because school is out of session for a few more weeks and most of the teachers are on vacation, Madame Ndiaye has agreed to meet me at a gas station instead of the school. I suggested it as a meeting place because it has one of the few ATMs in the neighborhood. I get there before her and withdraw the Mayfair Rotary Club's donation.

Her car pulls into the parking lot and she calls me over. I get in the passenger seat, and, feeling like a Mafia Don, hand her a thick envelope of cash. In it is an entire year's worth of good news from Mayfair Rotary.

"This will start the program off for the year and keep you going until the paperwork for the bank account is complete," I say. "Then we'll be able to wire the money directly to you."

She turns the envelope over in her hands, but doesn't peek inside. To count the money would be rude. After a couple minutes of silence, she bounces the envelope towards me, as if to show how weighty it is.

"Katie," she says. "You, Natalie, and Ling Ling have given the students a great gift, one so big that only God himself can pay you back." She leans over, opens the glove compartment and slides in the envelope. There is a serious look on her face until she pats the glove compartment closed, convinced of its security. Then she turns to me with a huge grin on her face.

"Things have changed, thanks to you three. Our students have so much more energy now and attendance in afternoon classes has gone up! Because the lines of socioeconomic status have been erased, there is a growing solidarity between all students. Students like Babacar now have a chance in school."

"Babacar?" I ask, taking the bait. I can tell Madame Ndiaye loves to tell stories.

"Babacar is eleven years old, the youngest of eight children. His father is a fisherman and his mother is a maid. Their family is extremely poor and because of his frequent absences, Babacar was taking two years to complete each grade. Eventually, his parents couldn't afford to raise him and an aunt offered to take him in. That was his first blessing.

"His second was that she enrolled him at *L'Ecole Primaire de Point E*. The stability and nutrition of a daily lunch has helped Babacar not only catch up to his classmates, but exceed most of them. He came to us dull and sullen and, in less than a year, he's transformed into a happy and bright boy. At the end of the school year, he said he was happy to visit his parents for the summer, but was going to insist he be sent back to his aunt's house for school.

"He told me he loves his school too much to leave now—especially the cooks!"

She laughs and tries to give me a sideways hug, made awkward by the small seats in the car. We talk for a long time about our families, the teachers at the school, Ling Ling, Natalie, and Monsieur Sane. When we say good-bye, she reminds me to thank all the generous people who've given money to her school.

"I will," I say, stepping out of the car. I wave as she drives away.

I am anxious to get to Yayeme and go to the bus station as early as I can the next day. As the bus travels through the countryside, I am surprised to see barren fields until I realize we are following the path of locusts that have been making headlines in the international news. Hundreds of thousands of these insects have arrived in Senegal from Mauritania and have wreaked havoc on the livelihood of farmers across North and West Africa. With their insatiable appetites, the swarms of locusts strip fields to bare soil in less than an hour. It's the worst invasion of locusts in fifteen years, and the destruction of all the year's crops before harvest threatens to bring famine next year.

I can see the swarms outside the bus window, hazy clouds of yellow moving slowly through the countryside. The voracious insects perch atop fields of millet plants that are waving in the wind. The stalks are about knee-high and remind me of a young cornfield in June in Wisconsin. We pass a low field of peanut crops, and where there should be green, I see only yellow.

One unfortunate locust has been removed from the swarm by our bus, and his flattened carcass is stuck to my window. He looks like a grasshopper on steroids. His abdomen is as long and wide as my middle finger and his yellow wings are the color of a banana peel a few days past its prime. His guts are smeared all over the window, their mass almost equaling the size of the bug. I had read that locusts must eat their weight in foliage each day to stay alive.

Eventually, we move ahead of their path, and the fields are green and lush again. Who knows why they choose the path they do, completely destroying one farmer's hard work and food source for the coming year and leaving the field of his neighbor untouched? The scene is reminiscent of a Biblical plague, and as I ponder the injustice of fate, I am reminded of Zator's wisdom: "Man plans, God decides."

Fimela's bus stop is marked by nothing more than a gasoline pump on one side of the road, and three vendors seated on the other side of the road selling dry roasted peanuts, sugary peanuts, and tea. I turn down the offers from several boys with a horse and cart for hire and excavate myself from the group of taxi drivers who've surrounded me. I buy a few packets of roasted peanuts from the grandmothers who've set up shop in the shade, practicing my Wolof. The impracticality of having a suitcase with no wheels in all the airports is now worth it; I strap my oversized backpack on my back and make my way down the dusty road.

The first hundred yards of the road out of town are littered with plastic bags of garbage, tossed on top of rotting fish heads with all the meat picked clean from their spines. Goats are grazing in the garbage, and I pick up my stride to avoid the smell.

Soon enough, I am walking through millet and peanut fields, which are now higher than I have ever seen them. They change the landscape completely, and a few times I lose faith that I took the right way.

Eventually, I see some of the permanent landmarks that mark my path. There is the grove of cashew trees with their distinctly weeping branches and large, waxy leaves. The last time I passed them, they hung heavy with cashew fruits, each the size of an orange, bright red and sweet. Each fruit bears only one nut, which sprouts from the far tip of the fruit.

This tree is familiar for another reason too; it is my first bathroom break. The bus from Dakar makes few stops on its five-hour trip. This cashew tree is the first thing large enough to cover me while I squat behind it, and the path is usually deserted enough that I don't have to worry.

A recent rain has wet the sandy path, so that it preserves the tire tracks and footprints of those who have gone before me. I follow them to where the fields end and the road is lined on both sides by families' property.

In the familiar house where the young mother lent me her son as a guide into Yayeme on my first visit, there is a clothesline holding clean laundry—faded T-shirts, vibrant dresses, and colorful squares of fabric that will be wrapped into skirts and head scarves when dry. From under the curtain of clothes, like a cast taking the stage, run three braying goats, ten squawking chickens, and four small children who are chasing them through the yard.

I anticipate what I will find when I arrive. Diène will probably be at the *campement*, perhaps drinking tea with Musa or other neighbors. I have only been able to connect with him once since I returned to the USA. It was a very short phone call with a static reception, but it was enough to tell him that I'd be coming back this week.

When Diène opens the gate to the *campement* and I see his face break into a smile, the months since I've seen him last evaporate.

"I've been waiting since you called," he said. "I was afraid you wouldn't come."

He takes my backpack from me and carries it over to my hut. Sure enough, sitting under the mango tree, Musa and a few friends are drinking tea.

"Katie," says Musa, standing to shake my hand. "We've all missed you." In his breast pocket is the pen I gave him the day that I left.

My first few days in Yayeme are full, with a constant stream of people coming to say hello, making me feel welcome again. They all remember my name, and I am terribly embarrassed because I have forgotten most of theirs. The villagers jokingly accuse me of forgetting them, something I will never admit to. To do so would be so rude, so un-Senegalese of me. I am anxious to find the right time to tell Diène the news, but it is hard to get him alone.

My chance finally comes one afternoon when the heat is so intense that everyone stays at home, finding sanctuary in shade and as little movement as possible. Diène and I have unrolled straw mats under the largest mango tree in the *campement* and are there trying to escape the heat. I am lying on my back, looking up into the braches that are thick enough to block the sky, and I can only see green. Mango season is long gone, and nothing decorates the branches but the long, wide glossy leaves. Even the bats have moved, taking up residence in another tree whose fruit is in season.

"Diène," I ask, "do you remember the writing contest I told you about?"

"Of course," he says. "The one you entered with a story about your first visit to Yayeme, right? How could I forget?"

"Yes—the one with the $1,000 prize for the author. Well," I feel my smile breaking, unable to contain it anymore. "I won! And as I promised, I am giving your family the money."

He looks at me and, for a moment, I wonder if he has understood. His dark face, which is often decorated by a bright smile, is stoic and unchanging. I can't read his thoughts. I know that the prize money is almost more than an entire year's income for him. His face is unchanged as he looks at me.

I want to scream out and overreact. But I stay still and patient, looking at his face. Then I notice the right corner of his mouth quivering, his lip slightly pulsing with excitement.

"Katie," he says, his voice surprisingly steady. "That is good news. That is very good news. It is good for my family, of course, but mostly it is good for you. Your story was chosen as the winner."

"Yes, thank you."

He is smiling now, and he looks up to the trees on the other side of the *campement*. "Do you see the top of the tree?"

I squint into the sky and look to where he points. The leaves of the tallest tree in the *campement* are the only leaves with any sunlight touching them; their shadow is cast on all the others. They glisten in the sun, waving white light back at me; I feel Diène take my hand.

"This is a sign," he says. "And some day we will be here and you will have news about your writing as big and bright as that tree."

"*Inshallah*," I laugh, tilting my head towards the cloudless sky with its infinite blue. I let the sunlight burn the image in my memory and believe.

Epilogue

Almost five years to the day that Natalie, Ling Ling, and I walked on the beach in Dakar and asked the question that birthed Project Japalé Gouné, we are on a conference call to discuss the latest email from Monsieur Sane. We had asked him to put together various budget scenarios of the cost to feed the entire school, rather than just the poorest students.

"Based on the cost of lunches per student," says Ling Ling, "and the school's income from their boutique, school garden, and participation fees from the students who can afford it, I think the project could be self-sustaining next year."

We check and double-check our calculations and conclude that our original goal of creating a lunch project that would some day be fully supported by the school is well within reach. We can almost taste it.

It took a long time to get to this point, and the journey was full of ups and downs and false starts. However, at the time of this book's publication, the school is serving 10,000 lunches each year to nearly 200 students who would otherwise go hungry. In the five years since we began the partnership with the school, we've worked together to devise ways that they can generate enough income to run the lunch program on their own. We are almost there.

All visitors to Senegal get enchanted with some part of its magic, and Ling Ling, Natalie, and I were no exception. For the three of us, working on the school lunch project when we returned home was an easy way to stay connected to a place that had captured our hearts.

When I returned to Wisconsin, I was lonely and lovesick and having a hard time breaking the habit of making friendly conversation with strangers in my daily life. While I acclimated back to the breakneck speed and material pursuits of the USA, I began to share my Senegal story with Rotary clubs all over the state. I went to thank them for the opportunity that their funding gave me, and hoped to show them that their investment in me, as an Ambassadorial Scholar, paid dividends far and wide. I did these talks with no expectation of anything in return, except that the audience would leave with a better understanding of Senegal and its people.

Yet, over the course of five years, these talks and the ones like it that Natalie and Ling Ling gave have helped raise nearly $40,000 for the school lunch project. A reminder that *ño ko bokk*, the sharing spirit, is not exclusively Senegalese. At some point, when we realized our project was here to stay, Natalie, Ling Ling, and I decided to ask those at the school to name the program. They decided on *Project Japalé Gouné*, which means "lending a hand to children" in Wolof.

From the beginning, and during the years of growth, we have maintained a clear vision of our goal: a school lunch program that was supported entirely by income-generating projects of the school. Our initial donation was only a jumpstart of capital that enabled the school to begin thinking big. It facilitated the opportunity to work together to create something good.

And yet, like the hunter chasing the monkey through the jungle, we had no choice but to move towards that vision step by step. *Ndank, ndank.*

These steps were as varied as our days. Holding monthly conference calls to manage the project. Maintaining email correspondence with the school. Writing donors to let them know how their money was making a difference. Analyzing financial statements and projected budgets. Soliciting advice from partners and experienced colleagues in the international development field.

For the most part, these steps led us closer to the goal. The first full school year we funded the lunch program entirely for a cost of just over $8,000. Each year since then, the school has created ways to earn income for the project. They rented out a room to a local shopkeeper. They planted a school garden and sold the extra vegetables. They started offering the lunches to students whose family could afford to pay a small fee. Each year, the school has contributed more to the project's total budget as we have contributed less. The past year, the school was able to run the lunch program at full capacity and it only required a $400 subsidy from us.

There were steps we took that didn't always lead us where we thought it best to go. I still remember the conference call with Natalie and Ling Ling where we'd thought we'd come to the end.

It was February of the first full year we funded the program, and the three of us had convened an emergency conference call because the school just informed us they had no money left for the remainder of the school year. The extra money we had raised was intended for next year's work, and we hesitated to give it to the school after they had strayed so wildly from the annual budget.

"Shit," I said after looking at the latest budget Monsieur Sane had sent us. "They are really burning through the money."

When we asked Monsieur Sane what had happened to the money, he was very honest. For one, the good meat they served in every meal was more expensive than anticipated. Second, they had loaned some of the money to help people in their school and community. After all, in Senegal, to have money and not share it was extremely selfish. So, when one teacher had an unexpected family death, they loaned her money for the funeral. Parents of a student who had fallen gravely ill were given help to pay for medical expenses. Families who had fallen on hard times were given some financial assistance. All of these were completely worthy causes, but also completely inappropriate uses of our money.

"I hate to risk the school lunch program failing," Ling Ling said, "but in a way, if we send more money, the program has already failed."

Understanding that our decision raised the risk of the school lunch program shutting down completely, the three of came to consensus: we would tell the school that we were not sending any more money for the remainder of the school year. In addition, we expected them to pay back the money that they had taken for unauthorized expenses. There were four months left of the school year, and they would have to figure out what to do on their own.

I hung up the phone that night wondering if we'd be hanging up the program soon, too.

Two weeks later, we got an update from Monsieur Sane. After he explained to the staff at the school that they were at risk of losing the lunch program, they all pooled their money to keep the program open. They scaled back the menu, alternating between heavy and light meals. On top of that, the teachers started making and selling tuna sandwiches to people in the neighborhood at lunchtime, earning enough money to pay back the program for the unauthorized expenditures. Not only did they save the project as it faced extinction, they embodied the proverb *nit nit ay garabam*. Man is man's best remedy.

I have never felt like the project was wholly ours, or that we were the ones making it happen. I feel more like we were simply conduits, coordinating the generosity of many people into a focused effort. I hope to continue to do so as more and more people learn about, and are compelled to help, the children of Senegal.

I left Senegal and returned to a place that I still don't feel is wholly home anymore. Productivity leads our days, we never have enough time to do what we really want, and people pass each other on the street without looking at one another. But I have kept parts of Senegal with me, in my spirit, heart, and even household. Two years after Diène took me to the Dakar airport, I picked him up at the Milwaukee airport, ready to start the next chapter of our life together. He was waiting outside of baggage claim on a snowy night, wearing a T-shirt and a look of sheer terror on his face. Love will drive you to do crazy things.

The greatest gift Senegal has given me is a deep sense of gratitude for my life. Not because I realize how much material comfort, luxury, and opportunity I have (although that is true). Rather, because the Senegalese taught me that no matter what life deals you, there is always something to be thankful for. If you believe that God is good and that his will is benevolent, you begin to see the evidence. By recognizing that, I was granted a tiny peek into the secret of happiness that exists in the hearts of so many of the people of Senegal.

PROJECT JAPALÉ GOUNÉ

Project Japalé Gouné began in 2003 with a shared idea that three Rotary Ambassadorial Scholars living in Dakar, Senegal could help students in their newly adopted community. Now it serves 10,000 lunches each year to low income students at our partner school.

To learn more about Project Japalé Gouné and how you can help, visit www.ProjectJapaleGoune.org

ABOUT THE AUTHOR

Katie Krueger has lived, worked, and written on four continents. An entrepreneur, Katie owns Gratice Press LLC, a writing and speaking company whose mission is to help people grow their dreams. She writes mostly grants, travel stories, and blog entries— all of which can be found online at www.KatieKrueger.com. She lives and writes in Madison, WI.

Katie speaks to audiences about the importance of international education. Past audiences have included Viterbo University, Bennett College, and Rotary International. If you are interested in having Katie as a speaker, contact her at Katie@findfunding.net.

GIVE WITH GRATITUDE ORDER FORM

Mail. Fax. Online. Send this completed form to:
Gratice Press LLC, *Attn: Katie Krueger*
525 Miller Ave #2, Madison, WI 53704
Fax: (720) 247-7955 Phone: (608) 234-0401
Katie@findfunding.net
www.katiekrueger.com/gratitude

PARTNER WITH KATIE TO SUPPORT LIBRARIES.

Purchase additional copies for $5 each to donate to libraries of your choice. No S&H. Books will be mailed directly to the library. Please list libraries you would like to support.

I would like _____ copies at $14.95 each = $_____
Shipping & Handling ($3/book) = $_____
WI Residents add 5.5% sales tax = $_____
Library donation @ $5 each = $_____
Purchase total = $_____

Payment Method
Checks payable to Gratice Press LLC. Credit card information below.

Name _____
Email Address _____
Phone Number _____
Address _____
City _____ State _____ Zip _____

Card Number _____
Expiration Date ___ /___ Card Security Code _____
On the back of your card, locate the final 3 digit number.